THE
NEW
REAL ESTATE
▲▲▲▲▲GAME

D0167163

215 9937

THE NEW REAL ESTATE GAME

BUILDING WEALTH
UNDER THE NEW TAX LAWS

HOLLIS NORTON

CB

CONTEMPORARY
BOOKS

CHICAGO

Library of Congress Cataloging-in-Publication Data

Norton, Hollis.
  The new real estate game.

    1. Real estate investment—Law and legislation—United
States—Popular works.   2. Real estate investment—
Taxation—Law and legislation—United States—Popular
works.   I. Title.
KF1079.Z9N67   1987   346.7304'37   86-32902
ISBN 0-8092-4794-1   347.306437
ISBN 0-8092-4577-9 (pbk.)

Contents

CHAPTER ONE

Dispelling the Myths About Real Estate Investing

Before you learn about real estate, how it works, and how to make money from it, you should know what's *not* true about it. The problem is that everybody's an expert. If you pulled into a filling station and told the guy pumping gas, "I've got this terrible pain in the right side of my head. What do you think I should do about it?" the station attendant would immediately say, "I'm not a doctor; go see a specialist and get it taken care of." And yet if you asked that same person about real estate investing, he would say, "Well, in my opinion, I would do this and buy that, buy this and sell that." People who know nothing about investing in real estate dispense advice anyway.

We are all victims of the "Uncle Charlies" of the world. They may be friends, family members, real estate agents, or others. It's not that what they tell you is wrong. In many cases it is totally true—within the limited sphere of their

1

knowledge. There is a whole world out there of unconventional ways to work with real estate that will make you a lot of money. The 1986 tax law will lower your tax bite on many of the high-profit areas presented in this book. Those who fear the new law will become the motivated sellers from whom you will be buying real estate.

This book takes you beyond the "Uncle Charlies" and introduces you to a whole new world of real estate investing. You'll learn the advantages of the motivated seller, how to get paid $200 to $300 per hour instead of $5 to $10, how to motivate yourself and set powerful goals, how to turn your local paper into a gold mine, and some powerful questions to ask sellers.

You'll learn how to write the offer in a way that protects you, the buyer. You'll read about ways to generate a down payment that don't involve cash. You'll learn ways to eliminate negative cash flow, such as by making the tenant your partner (equity sharing). You'll find out how to make tens of thousands of dollars using a simple lease-option technique. When you understand that a mortgage substituted for cash at the time of a sale is done on a one-to-one basis, and a mortgage sold for cash is done at a discount, you'll have found a source of immense profit.

This book tells you how to crank banks, and how to tell what a property is worth so you don't overpay for it. Since negotiation is involved, the book gives you some basic negotiating tips that will make you a lot of money. It tells you when to bring a partner in and how a parternship can be profitable for both of you. It shows you how to overcome the seller's objection to your buying without cash.

You're going to learn how minor fix-ups build wealth and what repairs to avoid like the plague. You'll enter the world of foreclosures, and you'll learn to buy property at a 35 to 50 percent discount for instant profits. You'll also meet professionals who can help you, and you'll get a specific plan to get started with. This book, if used properly, can make you a lot of money.

THE ULTIMATE MYTH

The ultimate myth (believed by many) is that buying real estate takes cash, good credit, financial statements, and perhaps cosigners. Baloney! For my first million dollars in real estate loans, I never qualified for a loan, nobody checked my credit, and nobody verified my income. I didn't do it in a single loan—I did it house by duplex by fourplex, until I was $1 million in debt. What I did, you can do. Later, this book shows you exactly how to do it.

You've got to stop listening to the Ned Negatives of this world, whose only reason for existence seems to be to keep the rest of us from getting anywhere. You may have to divorce yourself from the thinking of family, friends, peers, and anyone else who stands in your way. Don't worry—as soon as you start to climb up the ladder, they will be reaching to catch one of your heels. Those who once laughed will be begging to be included. Don't let anyone take away your dreams; they're yours, not somebody else's.

YOU MAY NOT LIKE WHAT YOU HEAR

Anyone can be wealthy. Notice this doesn't mean *everyone* will be wealthy. As a matter of fact, if I wrote 10 books or 20 or more, about 1 to 2 percent of the people in this country would be well off, and the rest of the population would be scratching out a living. Why is that? In this land of unlimited opportunity, where literally anyone can build wealth, most of the population lives with money problems.

To help you understand, I'll share an old story with you. A young man was searching for the secret to true happiness. He arrived at a town and was told by a local that a very wise man who lived on a nearby mountain knew the secret of true happiness. The young man got directions and set out to find the man on the mountain. Finally, in the distance, he saw an old man sitting in front of a hut. It took the young man almost an hour to reach the figure. He walked up, sat down, and said, "What is the secret of true happiness?" The old man looked into his eyes and replied, "Poverty, fasting, celibacy, and abstinence." The young man, not liking what he heard, glanced around and said, "Is there anyone else up here I can talk to?"

And here lies the rub. You may not like what you hear. Many people would say, "Do I have to give up beers with my coworkers after work in the summertime to go look at properties? Do I have to spend less time watching television? Spend less time with my family? Cancel barbeques? Give up some fun? Oh, you're talking about commitment. Gee, I thought you might have a magic lamp I could rub a few times, and a genie would appear and bring me wealth. I don't want to get that involved."

Does all that sound familiar? Does it sound like you? Have you figured out why you're not going anywhere? Anybody can become wealthy, but you will never build financial independence by accident. You will build it on purpose, or it will never happen to you. The price you must pay for financial success is far less than the price you have already paid for failure. You only have to get up off your ASSets and start to do it. This book will give you direction, a battle plan, and the mechanics of how to do it. There is an old saying that if you're going to lead a horse to water, start with a thirsty horse. If you're going to make it financially, you've got to get thirsty.

You might be wondering how you can get started. You might think you have virtually nothing to start with. But if you can learn to package situations, you can walk out of real estate closings with cash or notes even though you came in with nothing. This book teaches the exception to the rule that it takes money to make money. Hint: It doesn't have to be your money.

You must learn how to use debt as a vehicle to build wealth. There is a difference between constructive debt and destructive debt. Destructive debt is credit cards, charge accounts, living-over-your-head debt. Constructive debt is borrowing money for the specific purpose of making money with it. A real estate mortgage is always constructive debt.

Read on, and learn how to borrow money virtually without risk and to have the property, which you have little or no money in, stand as the only security for the debt. The greatest eliminator of fear is knowledge. When you take the time to train yourself, your financial wagon starts to roll.

CHANGE YOUR MINDSET

How much are you worth an hour? Whenever I ask that question, most of the answers I hear range between $5 and $20 an hour. Occasionally I hear an answer like $200 or $300 per hour. What's the difference? Why is one person worth $10 an hour and another person worth $200 an hour? The answer in one word is mindset. A wise person once said, "Everyone from the neck down is worth $200 a week." If you want to make more, you have to work from the neck up. You make a living with your hands; you build wealth with your mind.

None of this has anything to do with IQ or education. There are many educated derelicts, and I have met many millionaires with less than a high school education. Change your mindset, and you change your life.

Here's an example. If I told you to make $25,000 and gave you no time limit, what would you do? Many people would say, "Get a job, work about a year (plus or minus a few months), and I would have my $25,000." What if you gave me the same challenge? I would respond, "I'll go find a piece of real esate and buy it $25,000 under market. The day of closing, I would have made the money." If I could complete that task in 10 hours, I would have paid myself $2,500 per hour ($25,000 ÷ 10 hours). If it took me 20 hours, my earnings would plummet to $1,250 per hour.

What if you, a beginner, took 100 hours to complete the task? You would still be paid at the rate of $250 per hour ($25,000 ÷ 100 hours). What if you worked at a snail's pace, and it took you 200 hours to complete the task? You would still be paid at the rate of $125 per hour ($25,000 ÷ 200 hours). Are you starting to understand? If you want more money, don't rent your body out to an employer at $10 or $20 per hour. Work in an area that will reward you at the rate of hundreds of dollars per hour.

LEARNABLE BUSINESS

Real estate investing is learnable. Twelve years ago, I didn't know a house from a hill of beans. I was standing out in front of my first seller's house with knees knocking and a mouth so dry I could barely speak. I had to screw up all my courage to make myself walk up and knock on the door. Because of my nervousness, I messed up pretty badly. I sat in my car, made some notes of what I thought I did right and wrong, and went out again. The next time I was better. A funny thing happened by my ninth or tenth try. I surprised myself at how good I was getting (practice makes perfect). The sellers stayed the same, and I got better and better with each try.

Because real estate investing is learnable, you can start from anywhere. Twelve years ago I was living in a $200-a-month rented apartment, had never owned a home, had bad credit and erratic income, and was thousands of dollars in debt. Maybe you're just as bad off now. Anyone can do it, but you have to choose being one of those who does do it. The next chapter shows you how to get started.

CHAPTER TWO

The Five Steps to Building Wealth

If you follow the directions in this chapter for the next 30 to 60 days, you will find that drastic changes will occur in your life. You will get comments from your friends, neighbors, and coworkers. You will appear to be a changed person; in many ways, you will be. Your work output will increase, and your life will acquire direction. The strides you will take toward financial independence will be a by-product of those efforts.

It's important that you keep this chapter close at hand and continue to refer to it. Read this chapter several times before you proceed with the rest of the book. These are the building blocks upon which you will build your financial house. Each block is important; you can't leave one out.

STEP 1: GOAL SETTING

Setting goals is not important—it is imperative. Until you make a commitment, it is highly unlikely you will ever get off square one. And yet, this simplest of actions is the most overlooked by people who start to think about building wealth.

The other problem is that few people have any idea what good goals are and how to set them. In my lectures, people tell me they already have a goal. When I ask them what it is, they reply, "I've told all my friends my goal is I want to be wealthy." Or I might hear, "I want to be a millionaire."

Are these good goals? As a matter of fact, they are absolutely worthless. Take a look at the five components of a good goal, and then you'll understand.

Specific

A good goal must be specific. It must be a definable something that you will accomplish. "I think I'll buy some rental property" is not a good goal. "I will buy a minimum of two pieces of rental property" is better. It is measurable and precise.

Includes a Time Limit

To be any good, your goal must have a time limit for its completion. "I will buy a minimum of two pieces of rental property" has little value until you add time. If you add the three words "in one year," then your goal has value.

Compare this goal with, "I want to be wealthy." How long should it take to accomplish it? People could work on that goal after they're dead; it's not even limited to a lifetime. Do you see why the time element is so important?

Believable

For a goal to have value, it must be believable. "I will be

financially independent nine months from now" lacks credibility. If you believe you have as much chance of accomplishing a goal as you do of flapping your arms and getting airborne, you won't assign time to accomplish the goal. The result is you just won't work on it.

"I will buy $5 million worth of real estate in the next year" is something you won't work on. "I will buy two pieces of real estate in the next year" is something you will work on.

In Writing

To have value, your goals must be put in writing. A major university conducted a survey to determine why people are successful. They took leaders in this country and tracked them to see if there was some common denominator. The people came from all different races, colors, and creeds. The researchers could only find one common thread that ran through them all: All of these people had written goals, some as early as high school. How important it is.

In my lectures, I ask two questions. When I ask around 500 people, "How many of you have written financial goals?" I rarely see more than two or three hands go up. When I ask, "How many of you have written wills?" I see hundreds of hands. To wake up the audience, I say, "People, you're planning more for your death than you are for your life." Is this true of you also?

You change your life when you change your habits. You should have written goals as long as you live.

Displayed

For goals to remain vivid in your mind, you must see them daily. They must be placed in your home in an area where you can't miss them. Some examples are:

1. On your mirror in the bathroom—Chances are you

are shaving or putting on makeup every day, and you can't miss them.
2. On your refrigerator door—This is something you open several times a day.
3. On or over your desk or work area.

Keep your goals visible. A friend of mine wrote his goals on cardboard and taped them to the ceiling over his bed. He said, "The last thing I want to see at night before I go to bed is my goals. I want my subconscious mind to work on them while I'm asleep." He went a long way in a very short time.

STEP 2: MOTIVATION

As critical as having written goals is the battle to motivate yourself to work on them. This poses a problem in two areas: in the beginning, when you must retrain yourself to do things differently, and a few years into your program, when enough wealth comes to make you comfortable and you must remotivate yourself and redefine your goals in order to keep going.

Fortunately, many more aids are available than there were in the past. If you don't have a tape deck in your car, go down to a discount store and invest in the world's cheapest cassette tape recorder. This will let you use the dead time in your life, the time you spend driving to work. If you commute by train or bus or use a car pool, buy a small headset to give yourself privacy. Then go to a major bookstore. Almost all of them have a rack of cassette tapes. Pick out a tape on motivation, and develop the habit of playing that tape going to and coming from work. In a scant week or two, you will notice a difference in your work output.

The last chapter will give you a time-management plan that, combined with the tape, can easily double your work output. (And that's something your boss is bound to notice, which won't hurt you at raise time.)

STEP 3: VEHICLE

If you're going to build wealth, you've got to select a money-making vehicle. If you have a quarter to a half million dollars in cash, there are many ways you can make money. If you're starting with little or nothing (as I did), real estate is the only vehicle in which you can build wealth in a few short years (so you're young enough to enjoy it).

The problem is, it takes money to make money. You can't violate that rule. The good news is, it doesn't have to be your money. You can make as much money using borrowed money as if you were already wealthy. With real estate, once you've learned a few basic concepts, you will find it easy to control debt and use it as a vehicle to build wealth. And you can do it safely, securely, and with a whole lot of control— once you know what you're doing.

STEP 4: SPECIALIZE

If you're going to become successful, it's critical that you work an area. If you live in a city of any size, it's almost impossible to learn an entire marketplace. The bigger the city, the more imposing the task.

Localize yourself. Pick an area, perhaps your own neighborhood or one nearby, and become an expert in that area. You might take an area as small as 10 blocks by 10

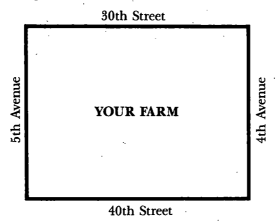

blocks, perhaps a square mile, and learn it. Call that your financial farm. You will work this area, and it will give you enough money to eliminate the need for you to have a boss.

STEP 5: LEARN YOUR MARKET

It's true that you can't recognize wholesale if you don't know retail. If I told you I could get you widgets for a dollar apiece, you would have no idea whether the price was good or bad. If I tell you that you can buy a certain house for $78,000 and you don't know the neighborhood is full of $100,000 houses, you will say, "Oh, really?" and go on to the next subject.

You must learn your market. Do it in a fixed period of time (remember goal setting). Look at houses for sale in your farm area.

Go into a couple of real estate offices that belong to MLS (multiple-listing service) and tell them you want to buy some rental houses in their area. Ask to see their Sold book. This is different than the listing book. The listing book shows what people are asking for property. The Sold book tells you what people are *paying* for property. Tell the agent you want to get an idea what property is selling for in the area.

Get in the habit of driving different routes to work. This will help you learn the area more quickly, and may alert you to a fresh sign put up by an owner. Learn rents in your farm. Use the Houses for Rent column in your newspaper, and play renter for a few days. Go out and see what your competition has to offer and what they are charging. Prepare yourself, so at the end of your 30- to 60-day period you will be ready to write offers.

SOME SELLERS ARE BETTER THAN OTHERS

If you're starting with little or no cash, confine yourself mostly to motivated sellers. A motivated seller is a person whose need to sell exceeds his or her need for cash. Little windows of time open up in a person's life when you can buy his or her property for little or no cash down. These windows are brought about by changes in a person's life.

Usually, these people are in transition. Transition can include divorce, loss of job, retirement, job transfer on very short notice. It can also come from excess work (leaving no time for effective management) or vacancy problems with no apparent solutions (there are unsuspected solutions). Some other motivated sellers include the following:

- Out-of-state owners (nothing creates motivation like remoteness)—If the property is vacant, this only makes their absence more pronounced. If the property is run down, send along a picture when you write the owner.
- A bad partnership—I bought an office building for $150,000 under market and less than 2 percent down from a disgusted general partner who, because of bad management, was having to feed the property. This problem had a two-word solution, "You're fired."
- Chicken Little—The owner starts to believe the 6:00 news that the world is really coming to an end and he or she had better sell quickly.
- Sickness—People become ill, especially as they become older. If the spouse looking after the property gets ill and the other has no interest, motivation builds quickly.
- Debts—I know it's never happened to you, but some people live over their heads, and they may be willing to discount their property in order to raise cash quickly.
- Income tax—The IRS is not patient, and people who need to raise cash to meet a deadline can give you a good price.
- Retirement—They've had enough. They want to retire and either travel or just take it easy. They want to live on the fruits of their labor. These people want

income and may be willing to carry back a mortgage on their property.

In the turmoil of the last few years in the job market and the shifting of people from area to area, opportunities present themselves daily. The next chapter discusses newspaper ads, including how to read them, reap a harvest, and discipline yourself to keep calling daily and weekly.

But the only person who's going to make you wealthy is you. If you'll pay some small dues for a few short years, you can live the rest of your life in a manner almost beyond your wildest dreams. After one of my lectures, a young man said, "Gee, I wish I were wealthy like you." I asked, "How much time did you spend this week working on building wealth?" He thought for a moment and then said, "None." I said, "You got out exactly what you put in: nothing. You want to reap without sowing. When you turn your attention toward wealth and care enough to assign time, wealth will come."

As a wise person once said, "You can make money, or you can make excuses; you just can't make both."

————————————————

Chapter Three

Reaping the Harvest
of the Classified Ads

You can become financially independent 10 times over using nothing but the classified ads from your local newspaper. The Real Estate for Sale section of the classifieds is an absolute gold mine.

Anyone who is renting an apartment can buy a home. If you limit yourself to the motivated seller described in Chapter 2 and are willing to keep calling and to keep asking, you cannot fail. There are too many people in trouble. You only have to find the right sellers, solve their problem, and you will be the proud owner of your first home or condo.

WATCH THE HEADLINES

Develop a habit of opening the classifieds first thing and scanning the headlines of the ads. The headline is the three or four words in bold print at the top of the ad. Here are examples of actual headings taken from newspapers:

MUST SELL	**PLEASE MAKE AN OFFER**
TRANSFERRED	**BRING ALL OFFERS**
NOTHING DOWN	**LITTLE DOWN**
$1,000 DOWN	**SELLER DESPERATE**
LEAVING AREA	**TAKE ADVANTAGE**
FACING FORECLOSURE	**ANXIOUS SELLER**
OWNER MOTIVATED	**DISTRESS SALE**
LOW DOWN—NO QUALIFYING	**MUST SELL NOW**
SELLING TODAY REGARDLESS	**MUST SEE NOW—**
	REDUCED $30,000

Recently, I answered an ad that said, OWNER DESPER-ATE. The first word in the ad was "Help!" Yet I still meet people who say, "If we could only buy a home." I can only assume these people never read the paper. If Attila the Hun walked up and looked like a prospective buyer, some of these sellers would drag him inside. You only have to look and act.

These properties sell. The problem is that when sellers become desperate, the sale usually takes place quickly. These opportunities have a short life span. In other words, don't do your hair, have a barbecue, go fishing, play golf, and then give them a call. You're going to hear, "Sorry, we sold it." Somebody who wanted to make money more than you did got there first. It is important that you move on these situations, that you sit down and put something in writing before a better offer walks in the door. If writing an offer scares you, it won't after you read Chapter 5. After one of my lectures, I spoke to a man who was from India. I have never heard worse English. He mispronounced so many words, you really had to focus your attention to understand him at all. He arrived in this country six years ago, speaking no English and virtually broke. He is now the proud owner of 42 rental houses and is quite well off. No wonder he didn't take time to learn English; he was too busy buying real estate. I can imagine the hours he spent poring over the paper, making calls, and trying to make himself understood. And yet so many people have no property or perhaps just their own home. What's holding you back?

OTHER INDICATORS

Let's look at some other indicators of good buys: assumable financing and price reductions.

Assumable Financing

There are literally thousands of FHA and VA loans you can take over, with no qualifying, at interest rates of 9 to 10 percent. When you have time available, call as many sellers with these loans as you can and feel them out. Use the telephone techniques described in the next chapter. Look for indications of willingness to carry back financing and willingness to accept little or no down payment. Don't be afraid to ask.

Price Reductions

Time is the greatest creator of motivation. Unsuccessful sellers, as they become motivated, may drop the price in order to hurry the sale. Requirements for down payments may drop at the same time.

A clever technique is to offer more money in return for soft terms (low down payment and low interest on the mortgage they are carrying). If the sellers reduced the property $20,000 below market, you might offer to give them back $10,000 of their reduction in return for terms. It could look like found money to them, and it will make your terms look more attractive.

READ BETWEEN THE LINES

You can find motivation in ads even though none is indicated. By learning to interpret a little, you can find bargains that other people looking for motivation may miss. Let's take three examples:

3 BR, 2 B home for sale—assumable FHA loan—Bob— 888-7777, 222-3333, 444-6666	Bought another home—don't need this one, 333-4444	3 BR, 2B home for sale, 888-9999. 4 BR, 3 B home for sale, 888-9999

The left-hand ad makes no mention of motivation, except for one thing. Bob sure doesn't want to miss your call. He gave you his work number, his home number, and probably his girlfriend's number. This is a subtle sign of motivation, and it is certainly worth a phone call.

The middle ad again contains no suggestion of motivation or that the sellers might be flexible on the down payment. Or does it? What is the principal need for cash on the part of a home seller (other than to pay a brokerage commission)? They need cash for a down payment on their next home. Not so with these people; they have already bought it. The other problem they have is two house payments, since the house they just moved out of and are selling is probably vacant. On your current salary, how would you like two house payments? If a few months have gone by, motivation could have set in.

The right-hand ad gives only one clue. There are two houses for sale, and they have the same phone number. Who sells two houses at the same time? Usually, a speculator. If he's selling more than one, he may have been hit by vacancies, be in a cash bind, and really need to sell. This is a person who, when backed into a corner, can become flexible.

Another thing I've had success with is calling broker/owner ads. Many people avoid these, fearing perhaps that the agent might take advantage of them. Nobody goes through large income swings like agents. It seems to be either feast or famine. They buy real estate in the feast and have to unload during the famine. You can catch one who is in a real famine. If the house is vacant, and there is a payment coming due that the broker can't make, he or she can become flexible. If you detected a problem, don't be afraid to write a very flexible offer. You can get yeses to some very strange offers.

RUN YOUR OWN ADS

If you have a few spare dollars, you might think about letting motivated sellers call you. You could run an ad like this:

> BEHIND ON YOUR PAYMENTS?
> SAVE YOUR CREDIT.
> CALL HOLLIS, 888-9999

A FEW MONEY-MAKING TIPS

The Sunday paper is normally your best source of finding motivated sellers. The problem is, there are a lot of people calling those ads on Sunday. Interestingly enough, the Sunday paper comes out on Saturday. The papers are different because the news changes, but the classified ads are the same. What if you picked up a copy on Saturday? If you're really motivated to make money, you could call the newspaper and find out where you could pick one up the earliest. Do a quick scan, pick out the most desperate ads, call, and make appointments for Saturday afternoon. You may have the best buy in the paper tied up before anyone else gets to it.

Keep a card file. Buy a batch of three-by-five index cards and a file box. Keep a record of calls you've made and the results. Organize your cards by phone number. People might change their ad, but they won't change their phone number. Glance at your records before you make the call. You may have a motivated seller who used to be semi-motivated, and you can call back like an old friend. "Hi, this is Hollis, I spoke to you . . ." Perhaps something you wrote down before may help you close the transaction. Every little edge helps.

Leave your number. If they seem somewhat motivated but not enough, leave your phone number. Say politely, "If your situation changes and you have to close quickly, give me a call. Perhaps we can work together." I received a call, over a year later, on an office building which I bought for less money and softer terms. The motivation had obviously increased.

OTHER WAYS TO LOCATE SELLERS

The courthouse is a great source of information. It will tell you who's getting divorced (possible sellers), who's getting married (buyers for your homes you can sell on soft terms), who's being foreclosed on, and the names and addresses of owners (they have to send the tax bills somewhere). Pay attention to out-of-state owners, since they are the most likely to sell (absence doesn't make the heart grow fonder with real estate). Write letters indicating you're a buyer. When you make a purchase this way, it's more than likely you're the only buyer and not competing with other bids.

Drive neighborhoods. Spend an extra 10 minutes a day and make a lot of money. To our financial detriment, most of us drive the same route to work every day. Take a map and lay out some alternative routes to work. Make a habit of driving three or four strange blocks per day. Look for abandoned houses. You've seen them. They're vacant, look run down, and have two feet of grass in the yard. When you have the address, the courthouse tax rolls can tell you who owns it. Neighbors, who want to get rid of an eyesore, will gladly help you locate them. Write the owners a letter: "Have you seen your property? [You, to be considerate, have enclosed a photo showing the worst possible angle.] To avoid a large loss, you should act immediately. . . ." You get the idea.

Buy sellers. Put out a reward. Tell your friends, neighbors, and coworkers what you're doing. Tell them you'll pay a $1,000 reward if they locate a motivated seller you buy from. When you pay, announce it to everybody—it can motivate others. The $1,000 amount is not etched in stone, but if you offer a pittance, you aren't going to motivate anyone.

Accountants know who owns real estate; they do tax returns. Tell yours you want to buy, and ask him or her to suggest it to others. Tell him or her to mention it to friends (other accountants?). Give your accountant some of your business cards to pass out. Don't forget to mention the reward. Explain that he or she will get something even if a friend gets the reward. Get people out on the street working for you.

Bankers know a lot of real estate investors who are in trouble and behind on their payments. The trick is to get them to tell you who they are. If you walked into a bank and said, "I'm looking for people who are behind in their mortgages. Do you have any?" you'd get a stuffy response. If you went to the same banker and said, "I buy problem mortgages, and I'll give you a good price. Do you have any?" you'd be amazed at the difference. A problem mortgage to a banker is one where the payments aren't current. Sit down and listen while the banker mentions some. Then say, "I'd be interested in buying them all, but first I'll need to look at the condition of the property" (a reasonable request).

When you have an address, what can you find out at the courthouse? The names of the owners. Contact them about buying their property (why not—they're motivated). Under no circumstance mention that they're behind on their payments or mention the banker. If they haven't been filed on yet (no one else is alerted), this is a perfect situation for you. A logical question to ask while you're talking to them is, "Are all the mortgage payments current?" A preliminary title report, explained later in this book, can give you the information you need to know.

A LAST POINT

When you've learned the seller's true motivation, you're halfway home. Ask questions; it's the only way to learn. Use the next chapter and practice, practice, practice.

Telephone Technique

A better name for this chapter might be Dialing for Dollars. Don't expect your phone calls to pay off immediately. You will probably start out quite poorly, as I did, and gradually build up to considerable ability on the telephone.

Part of what you are doing is information gathering, part of it is using a little psychology on the seller, and a little bit of it is selling. You have to do three things:

1. Determine the seller's needs.
2. See if the property fits what you're looking for.
3. Get the information you need to be able to write an offer.

If you're working full-time at a job, you have a limited amount of time. You don't have time to drive all over, just to walk around and look at properties you're never going to buy. Two or three effective minutes on the telephone will save you a lot of time and gasoline.

You should maintain as much warmth with the seller as possible. Don't call up and start firing out a long series of questions. First, state your name. People will say a lot more to a name than they will to a faceless stranger. You could start with, "Hi, this is [your name]. Are you the party with the home for sale?" When the seller answers "yes," find out his or her name. Get in the habit of using the name repeatedly during the conversation. People like to hear their own names. You could say, "And your name is?"

Let's say he's Sam Seller. The best way to warm people up is to get them talking. What subject would he love to talk about? You guessed it, his house. So, say, "Sam, could you tell me something about it?" Always have a pad and pencil and take notes. Some sellers tell you a little, and others are real talkers. The seller will sometimes give you information about price, square footage, the yard, the financing, and other things that you won't have to ask about later.

Read the ad a couple of times before you call, because you don't want to ask about what the ad tells you. If the ad says, "Desperate, will take anything," you don't want to ask, "Do you need a lot of cash?" While questioning the seller, you don't want to sound like someone who should be sitting in the corner wearing a pointed hat. Still, you're going to be nervous on your first few calls. You may ask something and then think, "Oh, that was dumb." Don't worry. This will pass with time. The more you practice, the better you get. The sellers, however, stay about the same.

QUESTIONS TO ASK

The next part of this chapter describes some good questions. It discusses why you ask them and what they're intended to accomplish.

Where Is the House Located?

Find out the area and the address of the house. You will

get a general area from the newspaper, since it groups
listings that way. The seller will generally tell you something like, "It's a little west of Jones Avenue and north of
Smith Street." If the seller doesn't volunteer the address, say,
"What is the address? I'll be out there today to look at
another property I'm interested in buying, and I'll drive by
yours at the same time. I want to make sure I like the area
and street you're on."

This plants a seed. Let the seller know there is competition for buyers and that you might reject the property out of
hand just from its location. This will put the seller in the
position of having to convince you this is a great property.

What Is the Price?

Assuming it's not in the ad, ask what the price is. You
must learn, over a period of time, to listen carefully to the
answers. The greatest salespeople in the world are all good
listeners. They really tune in when the other person is
speaking.

You can detect softness in the price just by the way a
person talks about it. If Sam says, "We are asking $76,000,"
that normally means he has already decided to take less. If
he says, "The price is $76,000," that statement generally
indicates firmness. As incredible as it may seem, sellers will
tell you what they are really willing to do during the course
of conversation, if you are only willing to listen.

If the price is listed, you could say, "Let's see, you're
asking $76,000, correct?"

There is a little game you can play here. After he gives
you the price, you could say, "Wow—$76,000! How did you
arrive at the price?" Notice that even though you haven't
said it, the seller assumes you think the price is too high.
The seller starts a mental process of lowering the price. To
the question "How did you arrive at the price?" you're
going to hear some very strange things. Beyond a ballpark
estimate, few sellers have any idea what their house is
worth. You may hear something like, "Well, Joe Parker

down the street sold his, and he got $76,000 for it." Joe may have had 1,000 more square feet and a half-acre more land, but that's a small point isn't it? Or, you may hear, "My sister-in-law's in real estate, and she says it's worth that." Don't argue. You can get to price later in the negotiation.

What Are the Existing Mortgages?

Ask what mortgages (or trust deeds) exist. Again, write it down. Look for high seller equity (25 percent or more) because, after all, the best lender in any city is the seller of the property. A motivated seller may be flexible on price, interest rate, and monthly payment.

Also look for a very high-amount loan you can easily assume and a seller with little equity. This works if interest rates at the time the seller got the loan were reasonable and the payment is not astronomical. The seller may be willing either to walk away from his or her equity or to carry it back in the form of a mortgage at very soft terms.

Look into price discounting as described in my first book, *How to Make It When You're Cash Poor*. You can get the seller to give you an 18 percent discount on the price of the house (see the example given in that book).

What Are the Payments and Interest Rates?

Learning the seller's payments and interest rates gives you a clue as to whether the house is feasible. Avoid high existing monthly payments on the first or second mortgage. With high payments, the property won't work either as a rental or in an equity-share situation. The exception to this is buying the house way below market and having a new loan lower the payments (assuming current rates allow it).

Check that the payments at least cover the interest. Mulitply the loan amount by the interest rate and divide by 12. For example, $70,000 \times .1 \div 12 = 583.33, the interest-only payment on a loan of $70,000 at 10%. If payments are less, some unpaid interest may be due to the former seller. Normally this would be true only if the mortgage was carried back by the former seller of the property. It's just something to be aware of.

Are the Loans Assumable?

Be careful here when asking whether the loans are assumable. The seller may tell you they are. For example, a seller may say a second mortgage is assumable because it is being carried by the person who sold it to her. She knows the first mortgage is assumable because she called her lender, and the lender said, "Yes, it's assumable."

Lenders have bastardized the word *assumable*. To the lender, it means you pay a higher interest rate, a higher monthly payment, loan points, bank fees, and the lender checks out your total history. If all that happens to be to the lender's liking, then you can take over the mortgage. If the seller says the financing is assumable, you might ask, "How do you know? Have you read the mortgages?"

Most conventional mortgages today contain the infamous Clause 17 (so named for its numerical position in the List of Clauses), which gives the lender the right to call the loan if the house is sold. The only way to tell if a mortgage is assumable is to read the mortgage.

Is the Loan FHA or VA?

A good follow-up question would be whether the loan is an FHA or VA loan. These loans are the federal government's gift to the real estate investor—loans with Federal Housing Administration insurance and Veterans Administration guarantees. You must be a veteran to get a VA loan, but anyone who qualifies can get an FHA loan. The good news is that anyone can take over either type of loan by simply signing his or her name and paying a $45 transfer fee. To join the Army, you must be warm and walking, but you only have to be alive (warm) in order to assume an FHA or VA loan. You could have lost your job, been bankrupt, or established a credit report that makes Freddie Flake look good, and you can still take over an FHA or VA loan. If you can get the seller to carry back all or most of his or her equity in the form of a mortgage, you could buy a hundred homes in this manner.

Why Are You Selling?

Asking why the seller is selling won't necessarily get you the whole truth and nothing but the truth, but it is a critical question. It can give you great insight into how motivated the seller really is. If a husband left on a job transfer to a different city a couple of months ago, a wife left behind might start wondering how pretty the women are in that other city and can become very motivated. With winter coming, retirees dreaming of Florida or Southern California can become very flexible. A couple who have bought a second home, still have the old one, and find that both house payments are beyond their capacity to pay would be very glad to hear from you.

Again, train yourself to listen. Don't be afraid to ask additional questions. When they make a statement, you ask, "Did you mean————?" The more the seller discloses, the better your chance of buying that house. You'll make a lot more money with your ears than you will with your mouth.

If We Come to Terms, How Soon Would You Be Able to Close?

If you ask how soon the seller can close, you get him or her thinking, "Here is a serious buyer. If I can satisfy this buyer, we can get rid of this house."

The nice part about this question is that there are no bad answers. You get free motivation with answers such as "anytime" or "as quickly as possible." Yet you can work with much longer periods of time. If, for instance, the seller said, "We are building a new home, and we can't move for four months," you could say, "That's OK; I'm an investor and I'll rent the house back to you until you're ready to move." The fact that you're solving their problem for them could be additional motivation to give you flexible terms.

What Do You Need from the Sale?

After you ask the seller what his or her needs are, sit back and listen. The seller is going to give you valuable information; drink it in. The seller could show flexibility by indicating a willingness to lend you a major portion of the down payment by carrying back a second mortgage. The seller will indicate what he or she wants for a down payment (not necessarily what he needs, just wants).

Ask questions if you're not sure what the seller means or if you want more information. You'll be amazed, after only a few weeks, at how much better you get at this. It's like a game in which you, through practice, get better and better.

What Will You Do with the Down Payment?

Asking sellers what they're going to do with the down payment is likely to provoke hostility. Especially at first, you'll probably feel uncomfortable asking because you feel you're butting into other people's business. Although it is a necessary question, you can soften it a great deal. You might try something like, "Sam, I'm a real estate investor. When people tell me they want cash for a down payment, in many cases it's to purchase something they want, or to take care of an obligation of some kind. I'm very creative, and I've been able to solve many of the problems they have in another manner. Tell me, what do you plan to do with the down payment?" This greatly softens the blow and can get you a response from the seller.

Here are some creative cases where the investor was able to solve the seller's problem without using cash.

Case 1: The seller, an elderly lady, insisted she had to have $12,000 for a down payment on a very nice house. Upon being asked what she intended to do with the money, she said her husband had gotten sick and died, and she had to pay a $12,000 hospital bill. The investor, a creative person, said, "If I could take over your hospital bill, would that be satisfactory as a down payment?" The woman said, "Fine." The investor then went to the hospital and found the collection department. He said, "I'm here on behalf of Mrs. So-and-so, who owes you $12,000. Would you rather have someone on the bill who was capable of paying it, or would you rather have her owe it to you?" He found they much preferred a stronger person. He said, "I'm that person." He then did a wise thing. He didn't tell them how he would pay it, he asked them what was the minimum payment they would accept on a monthly basis. The woman in charge referred to a book she had and replied $150 per month. That's how the investor got a loan of $12,000 to make his down payment on a piece of property. Even better, no one mentioned interest. He got an interest-free loan in the process, all from asking one question.

Case 2: A cash-poor young man was talking to an older couple about buying their home. They were more than willing to give up an obvious $10,000 in equity, but they had to have $2,000 cash. The young man asked about their plans and found out they were from a European country, had come here to live, and discovered they preferred to return to their native land. The $2,000 was for the airline tickets. When the young man asked when they wanted to leave, they replied sometime within the next two months.

He went to the airport and found out that, due to a current fare war, by buying more than 30 days in advance, he could get two one-way tickets to the country for about $800, which he bought using his credit card. Returning to their house with a quitclaim deed, a notary (for the document), and the tickets, he offered the couple the tickets in exchange for the house. They accepted. He graciously let them remain in the house, rent-free, until they left six weeks later. Obviously, he ran a title search to verify that what the couple was telling him was true. Isn't it interesting that all parties got what they wanted? Ask the question!

Case 3: Another investor, confronted with a $3,000 down payment, which he didn't have, found out the sellers wanted the money to buy new furniture for the house they were buying. He was able to secure what they wanted, using his Sears credit card, and was able to purchase the house without using his cash. You can, in some cases, give them what they want, just not in the way they expect it.

TOUGHER QUESTIONS

You'll also need to ask some more difficult questions.

How Long Have You Had the Property for Sale?

Inquiring how long the seller has had the property for sale isn't in itself a tough question, but it is a lead-in for the next two questions. You want to get a frame of reference of how long the seller has been fighting the problem. Time is almost an automatic catalyst to motivation. If you've ever tried to sell a house, for whatever reason, and months went by and nothing happened, you know just what I mean.

How Many Offers Have You Had?

When you ask how many offers they've had, you'll be amazed at how many people tell you "none." After the parade of lookers through the house, nobody came back to write an offer. They may be wondering whether anyone is ever going to write an offer. If a long time has gone by, you may look like a floating log to a drowning man.

Why Did You Turn Them Down?

If a seller says he or she has had an offer, ask why the seller turned it down. This will tell you what the seller found objectionable in the offers (perhaps you can adapt yours). You can find out whether the seller is stuck on either price or terms.

A wise investor found a seller who was adamant about getting a price of $100,000 for his property; in fact, the seller had told his friend he was going to get it. Now, the investor (and many of his friends) knew that the property was not worth a dime more than $95,000. The investor sat down and wrote an offer for no cash down and using a mortgage for the seller's equity at a very low interest rate over a long period of years. The seller accepted; he was stuck on price. You can bet that, out on the golf course next week when he was asked if he sold the property and what price he got, he replied, "Yes, and I got $100,000 just like I said I would."

What did the investor give him? Bragging rights. And the investor got what he wanted: great terms. Years from now, when that property has doubled or tripled in value, the investor won't care that he paid a little too much for it.

MONEY MAKERS

Because of the opportunities they reveal, some questions are great money makers.

Do You Have Any Other Properties for Sale?

There are three appropriate times to ask whether the seller has other properties for sale:

1. When you have closed on the seller's first property
2. When you have firmed up a close and feel you have good rapport with the seller
3. When you have decided the property in question, for whatever reason, is not something you are going to buy

Not asking this question can cost you a lot of money, and you will never know you have lost it. Leaving a closing where he had bought a house on very soft terms from a motivated seller, an investor casually asked, "Do you have any other properties you want to sell?" The seller replied, "I've got 11 other houses; would you like to buy them the same way?" The investor, after recovering from his shock said, "Yes." He got 12 houses instead of 1, and if he had never asked the question, he wouldn't have gotten the extra properties. It might have taken him years to find 11 properties he could buy on such favorable terms.

Do You Know Anyone Else Who Might Have a Property for Sale?

Find out about the friend, neighbor, or in-law who wants to sell a property. This gives you access to real estate that hasn't been offered or advertised. You get first crack at it, and it only takes a few minutes to ask whether the seller knows others who might sell their property.

Do You Know Why They Want to Sell?

Asking why these people want to sell is such a lovely question. I asked this once, and the man replied, "My neighbor lost his job, is two payments behind, and is desperate to sell." Didn't that knowledge put me in a great position to negotiate? What chance do you think I had of learning that from the neighbor? Third parties will tell you many things about people that you would never learn from them.

OTHER TIPS
What Else to Ask

Some other things to know about the house are square footage, number of bedrooms and baths, garage (one or two), whether there are fireplaces or a family room (these add value), whether appliances are included. Also ask the age of the house itself, the furnace, and the roof. A 15-year-old house with the original roof is going to have a major expense in a few short years. Take this into consideration when you discuss price.

The Farm-out System

It would be nice to report that getting the paper and making these calls and asking these questions is going to be fun, but it's far from that. You will, after a while, look forward to it like you look forward to crabgrass and boils.

However, all is not lost. As you acquire wealth, you can hire help. If you prepared a sheet of paper listing all the things you wanted to know, you could hire part-time college kids, or whomever, to sit by the phone and go through the mundane process of getting the knowledge you need.

There is also a second benefit. What we don't like, we tend not to do; we just put it off. The kids will make the calls when you won't. Why? Because it's their job, what they get paid for. Think about it. How many things do you do at work that you don't enjoy? You do those things because they're your job. You don't put them off, you just do them. As soon as you can afford it, farm out the jobs you don't enjoy.

Don't Be Overwhelmed

You might set a goal for the number of calls you will make, such as 20 calls per week. Be sure to keep a running tab, so you will always get in the required number. In 50 weeks you would have made 1,000 calls. By then you certainly will have bought some property.

You're not going to get all these questions asked, especially when you first start. Do what you can. It's only important that you get started. Keep rereading this chapter, and it will help you grow.

CHAPTER FIVE

Strategies for Writing Offers

In the last decade I have traveled all over this country and spoken to literally hundreds of thousands of real estate investors. In the process, I have answered thousands of real estate questions and have possibly heard every fear and objection you might have as a real estate investor. One of the major drawbacks to getting started is fear of writing an offer. This is mainly brought about by a lack of understanding of what an offer form really is and how to protect yourself when you're writing one. The statement across the top, **This is a legally binding contract,** doesn't help any. For some, that's like reading the sign across Dante's Inferno: Abandon Hope All Ye Who Enter Here.

Twelve years ago I didn't know a house from a hill of beans, and a real estate contract was strange and frightening. But all of these skills are learnable. Your job required that you learn some skills in order to stay employed. You learned them because you wanted to keep your paycheck. If you are as motivated about becoming financially independent, you will find that these skills are no harder to learn. Why not take the time to learn skills that might make you a quarter million to a half million dollars?

This chapter will acquaint you with an offer form and at the same time teach you how to protect yourself. You must understand that real estate brokers represent sellers. (The agent represents the person who pays him or her.) Even if another broker brings you to the seller's broker and your broker shares in the real estate commission, your broker becomes a cobroker representing the seller. Many buyers don't understand this. It just makes sense that an offer form used by a broker would tend to favor sellers. That's OK as long as you recognize it.

A TOUR OF THE OFFER FORM

A simple solution is to add clauses and additions to the contract that will turn it into a buyer's form, something that protects you, the buyer. Moving through an offer form from top to bottom, the following discussion gives you some things you'll want to add.

After Your Name

After your name as buyer, write "and/or assigns." The word *and* gives you the right to bring in a partner. A partner can solve two main problems. He or she could provide any cash needed for a down payment in return for, say, one-half ownership of the property. If only a small amount of cash is needed, you might offer one-quarter interest or less. If your partner is in a higher tax bracket than you, he or she could pay any negative cash flow on the property. With the tax benefits provided by the partner's share, he or she could make part of the negative payments with tax dollars.

The word *or* (in "and/or assigns") lets you sell the property to a third party, put cash or a mortgage (or both) in your pocket, and walk away. By putting together a simultaneous closing, you could use the other buyer's cash for a down payment, pass your share of the closing costs on to the other buyer, and use none of your own money. There is no limit to the creative ways you can make money in real estate.

Liability Limits

Limit your liability on the mortgage. In many states, if something goes wrong and the property is sold at a loss, the mortgage holder (mortgagee) can get a judgment against you to cover his or her losses. The mortgagee can then take your other assets. Have each property stand on its own; if you buy ten and one goes bad, you don't want it to drag five more down with it.

You can protect yourself by adding an "exculpatory clause" to your note and mortgage. Exculpatory is a fancy legal word that means freedom from blame. The clause might read something like, "The liability of this note [mortgage] shall be the building itself and shall not extend beyond it." Check with your attorney on the wording.

This works especially well with seller financing. What if the seller objects to the clause? You might say something like, "What? You mean the property isn't worth what I'm paying? What's wrong with it? What haven't you told me?" Then *shut up!* The next person to talk loses. The seller has to defend the property and may end up giving you the clause to prove there is nothing wrong with the property.

Also limit the contract liability. Remember, you are signing a legal contract and you might be sued for specific performance if you don't buy the building. Control this by adding a clause to the contract that limits the amount of damages to the earnest money deposit (which you make as small as possible).

If a broker says the seller wouldn't consider it without a large earnest money deposit, you might consider an interest-free note between you and the seller due at the closing on the property. If no closing takes place, the note is never due. Any broker worth his salt will have a liability-limiting clause in his or her contract; however, don't assume—look for it. If you're dealing directly with the seller, be sure your offer form has one.

Control vs. Buy

Has this ever happened to you? You found a really good buy, but being a person who likes to think it over, you looked at it for a couple of days. When you called up to tell them you'd take it, you were told it had already been sold. Well, that doesn't have to happen to you anymore. You just have to understand the difference between controlling a piece of property and actually committing to buy it.

You control a property by writing the offer in the normal manner and then adding some escape clauses, or "weasel" clauses. These clauses, until they are satisfied or removed, allow you to walk away from the contract. In fairness to the seller, there should be a time limit on exercising the clauses, say seven to ten days. This should give you plenty of time to check out the property and see if you really want to buy it. Meanwhile, it's tied up on a contract (assuming the seller signs your offer), and no one can steal it away from you.

Some escape clauses I like are:

- *Subject to inspection and approval in writing by the buyer* (a reasonable request)
- *Subject to buyer's inspection of books and records and approval in writing* (a necessary clause for income property)
- *Subject to approval by buyer's attorney* (your attorney will be glad to disapprove it, especially if you tell him or her to)

When you understand the difference between control and buy, you won't let the bargains get away from you. The greater the bargain, the more pressing the need to tie it up on a contract. You have learned a valuable lesson when you have learned you can't "steal" in slow motion.

Right to Extend the Closing

If you have a broker handling the transaction, he or she should have a 30-day extension clause in the offer form. The broker doesn't want to lose a commission because some of the paperwork didn't get done.

If you are dealing directly with the seller, you should have an extension clause in your contract. If you are trying to find a partner with the cash you need to close, an extra 30 days could be a lifesaver. You might get a broker's contract and use the broker's clause, substituting "buyer" for "broker" in the clause.

Negative Cash Flow

Eliminate negative cash flow. Later, this book will give you many ways to eliminate negative cash flow. Negative cash flow is much more a knowledge problem than it is a problem of the price of real estate. When you have alternatives, you don't have to accept what people try to hand you.

Extension Clause

An extension clause is especially good when you are working with balloon mortgages. (A balloon mortgage is a lot of equal payments followed by one terribly large final payment.) If your balloon comes due in a tight-money market with high interest rates and high origination points for new loans, you don't want to go out in that marketplace and shop for money, which places you at the seller's mercy.

An extension clause gives you room to breathe and wait for the rates to come back down. It might read, "If, in the buyer's opinion, when the seller's mortgage comes due, the current mortgage marketplace does not give a reasonable rate, seller agrees to grant to buyer a period of 18 months to acquire financing to cash out the seller. The original interest rate and payment shall prevail during this period. Buyer agrees to notify seller in writing 30 days before due date of his or her desire to exercise this option." Again, check with your attorney on the wording.

Who decides if the money market is too high? You do; it's your option. If the seller objects to the clause, you might say, "I couldn't possibly accept a balloon mortgage that short unless I had an out. Would adding more years to the balloon mortgage be better for you?" As before, be quiet and let the seller speak first. Whatever the seller chooses is good for you.

INTO ACTION

Go through this chapter at least once more, and do it while you're holding an actual offer form in your hands. The chapter will help you understand the form, and vice versa. It should take a lot of the fear out of writing contracts and enable you to get started.

Remember, you'll find real estate because you're looking for it, and you'll buy it because you're writing offers. Nothing will ever happen until you start to write offers. There are a lot of bargains out there. None of them is going to run up and bite you; you're going to have to beat the bushes and find them. Good hunting!

FOOD FOR THOUGHT

Under the new tax law, when you buy investment real estate (improved property), the government lets you pay less income tax. You get an artificial loss of up to $25,000 for your self-managed property on your income tax return (see Chapter 7). You get this from an investment that goes up in value (appreciates) and that someone else (the tenant) is buying for you. The only question is whether you can afford *not* to own real estate.

CHAPTER SIX

The Closing: Tips on Saving Money

One of the major loss areas for amateur investors is closing costs. Amateurs don't understand these costs, and they stare helplessly at a statement of charges before they sit down and write a check. When they ask why they have to pay for a particular item, they hear, "That's the way it's done," or, "That's conventional." Baloney! Nothing is conventional. If you pay attention, you will find you're paying a lot less of the closing costs, and the other person is paying more.

INVITE THE OTHER PERSON TO PAY

There is nothing wrong with inviting the other person in the transaction to pay all the closing costs. If you're the buyer, you write the offer, "Seller to pay all closing costs." In a normal transaction you will meet a lot of resistance to that proposal. When you are dealing with motivated sellers, you will find that some of them will accept it.

If they resist it, you can use paying your share as a

bargaining chip. You might say, "I'll be able to pay half if you lower the interest rate on the second mortgage you're carrying by 1 percent." Always ask. The worst thing that will happen to you is you're going to break even. You'll end up paying exactly what you would have paid anyway.

TITLE INSURANCE

When you are transferring title in real estate, a policy of title insurance is a major expense. Normally, the seller pays the cost of insurance, but there are exceptions in some areas of the country. Forget conventions. If you're the seller, the buyer pays. If you're the buyer, the seller pays. Write it in the contract that way. If, for instance, a buyer liked the rest of your terms enough, he or she might accept in order to get the property, even if it means paying for the title insurance.

Binder Policy

If a property sells within a year or two after the last title insurance policy was issued (after the last sale), the title insurance company has little research work. They have a way of collecting a little more in front and giving you a great savings down the road. For a premium paid (in front), you will only have to pay the difference between what the property sold for last time and what it's selling for now.

Normally there are one- and two-year binders:

- One-year binder—Pay 110 percent of normal premium; for a $1,000 policy, you would pay $1,100.
- Two-year binder—Pay 120 percent of normal premium; for a $1,000 policy, you would pay $1,200.

In the first case, if a property was sold for $200,000, and sold six months later (up to a year) for $250,000, you would only have to pay title insurance on the second sale as if it were a $50,000 property ($250,000 minus $200,000). It would mean a significant savings. In the second case, the only difference is that you would have two years to sell and just pay the difference.

If you're buying and the seller is paying for title insurance, you write in the contract: "Seller to provide a two-year binder policy of title insurance." The seller would then pay the extra premium, and when you turned around and sold the property, you would pay a very small title insurance fee (the difference in price) as the seller. This works great when you're doing turnarounds—buying a property, fixing it up, and reselling it. You could save thousands of dollars over the next few years. Even if you had to pay the extra premium (the 10 or 20 percent), it's still a good deal for you.

Your state should have binder policies if it has title insurance companies. Call your local title company and ask, "Do you have binder policies?" If they say, "yes," ask, "How much extra do I pay, and what do I get?"

Why Title Insurance?

Title insurance is money well spent. In many states it is almost impossible to transfer a title without it. It covers three basic areas:

1. It insures that the person who is selling has the right to sell.
2. It insures that the buyer gets all rights to the property that he or she is paying for.
3. It insures against unforeseen claims.

A couple bought a piece of land from the wife's uncle for $20,000. Her brother, an attorney, searched the title, and it was clear. The sale went through, and the deed was transferred. Two months later, the couple learned there was a tax lien on her uncle. The IRS seized the land, sold it at an auction, and there was nothing the couple could do. And she was dealing with *relatives*. Enough said?

THE PRELIMINARY TITLE REPORT

A preliminary title report (prelim) is *not* title insurance. It conveys information, nothing more. It will tell you:

• The status of the taxes
• The assessments
• The number, amount, and creditors of any loans against the property
• The existence of other liens, such as mechanics', or IRS liens
• Rights-of-way or easements

Prelims are useful in certain circumstances. For instance, if you were buying a house from a couple who wanted to take $500 and quitclaim (give) the property to you, you might want to know whether what they were telling you about the property was true. A prelim could tell you without your spending a lot of money.

Prelims cost $40 to $50. If you're doing a lot of them, buy 10 in advance and get a discount from the title company. If you are doing closings through the title company, you may get a bonus of looking at the records without having to pay for a prelim. If you don't ask, you'll never get it.

VOLUME DISCOUNTS

Whether you're closing through an escrow company or an attorney (depending on your state), understand that everybody likes volume. Volume, in any marketplace, demands a discount. If you can offer 15 or 20 closings a year, people should be glad to work with you at a reduced rate. The only way to find that many closings, unless you're a prolific buyer, is to join a group, be it the apartment owner's association, investment club, or whatever. If they haven't already set up a common discount-closing person, bring it up and work on the committee that organizes it. There is a lot of money to be saved.

Chapter Seven

The 1986 Tax Act, or the Government Giveth and the Government Taketh Away

The 1986 tax act. "It means real estate is doomed," several investors have said. Baloney! All Congress did was change the rules on the playing field and all that means is you have to make some adjustments in your investment strategy. Let's look at the changes first, and then we'll look at new ways to profit under the changes.

THE CHANGES

Depreciation

The 19-year straight-line depreciation of a property (as well as accelerated depreciation) has been removed. You are now allowed 27½-year straight-line (an equal amount taken each year) for residential property and 31½-year straight-line depreciation for all other property. Depreciation can be used to offset income from real estate but cannot be used to offset income from other sources (salary, interest income, etc.), with one notable exception. If you are actively in-

45

volved in the management of your property, you can use depreciation to offset other income up to a maximum amount of $25,000 (using the new depreciation schedules).

The key is to make sure you are in compliance. Sit down with your CPA or real estate tax attorney (or both) and work out how active you need to be in order to comply with the new law. This "special" deduction is phased out when your income reaches $100,000, but that should not come into play for 99 percent of you reading this book.

Let's take an example to calculate your write-off. A $100,000 rental house is sitting on a $20,000 piece of land. You can't depreciate land (the IRS won't allow it), so subtract the $20,000 land value from the $100,000 total, leaving an $80,000 house to depreciate. Use the new schedule, which is 27½ years, so divide $80,000 by 27½ years and come up with a $2,909 write-off per year. You would need between eight and nine $100,000 rental houses to reach your maximum write-off of $25,000.

You may be able to use this deduction to keep your maximum income tax bracket at 15 percent.

There is a little bonus in the arrangement. Depreciation not allowed to be used can be "stored" and used to offset future income from real estate up until the time you sell the investment.

Interest on Mortgages

Interest on mortgages for investment property can be used to offset income from the property itself, but it can't be used to offset other income. An exception applies to property purchased before the president signed the bill into law in 1986. On those properties, the interest deductions are phased out under the following rule:

1987	65 percent deduction allowed
1988	40 percent deduction allowed
1989	20 percent deduction allowed
1990	10 percent deduction allowed

These phased-out deductions can be used to offset other income. Interest on the home you live in and a vacation home or second home is still fully deductible. There is a cap on interest deduction when you refinance your home. The deductible part of interest is limited to the original purchase price plus any improvements. However, you may deduct interest above this amount if the refinance money is used for education or medical purposes. If you like a little humor, tell someone this law is a tax-simplification act.

Income Tax Brackets

The year 1987 will be a phase-in year, and there will be a total of 4 tax brackets with a top rate of 38 percent. If you are reading this book before 1988, you should sit down with your CPA and do some tax planning for this interim year. Starting in 1988, there will be 2 income tax rates, 15 percent and 28 percent, depending on whether your income is above or below $17,850 (single) or $29,750 (married and filing jointly).

There is a 5 percent surcharge on some income brought about by the phasing out of the 15 percent rate (as income increases) and elimination of personal deductions. The lowering of the tax rates doesn't mean you shouldn't invest in real estate, it just means you should do it differently. A little later, this chapter will look at what to do.

Capital Gains Tax

The special tax treatment of capital gains has been eliminated. Profits from a real estate sale will be taxed at the same rate as other income (regardless of how long the property is held before sale). The bad news is you're going to pay a higher rate. The good news is you don't have to hold property after you buy it just for tax considerations. You can now find below-market property and sell it immediately and take your profit. You can be less in the business of managing property and more in the business of making money from it.

Property Tax

Property taxes are still deductible. This means a portion of the property tax is to be paid with your income tax dollars.

SHORT-TERM WEALTH BUILDING

Now look at investment strategy. If you're in a 15 percent tax bracket, it doesn't make much sense to run out and shelter your income. Since you're in such a low tax bracket, run out and increase your income; you'll be paying such a low tax rate, not only on your current salary, but also on the extra money you earn. As you earn more, and your tax bracket creeps up to 28 percent (or if it's there now), you can look at retaining some rental houses that you buy and manage, and use the depreciation to keep your taxable income at the 15 percent level. Some ways to generate extra income include:

- *Wealth-building fixer-uppers*—Buy a house under market that needs paint and a little fixing up, upgrade it, and sell it for a profit. Take your profit in the form of cash or interest-bearing notes. Either way, you're going to have low tax rates on the extra income. See Chapter 16 for more details.
- *Lease-Options*—Find a lease-option at payments below market rent, get a right to sublet and rent for market rent, and create an instant cash flow for yourself of as much as several hundred dollars per month. See Chapter 10 for more on lease-options.
- *Mortgage Discount Techniques*—Create cash (if you don't have it) by refinancing your home or getting a partner with cash. Buy discounted mortgages and

create returns for yourself of 20 to 40 percent per year. Again, you're raising your income and paying low taxes on that extra income. Mortgage discount techniques are covered in greater detail in Chapter 11.

- *Fortunes in Foreclosures*—Buy houses at various stages in the foreclosure process below market and resell them at market. Again, take your profit in cash or mortgages and live better on the extra income. See Chapter 15 for more details.
- *Miscellaneous Money Makers*—Use wraparound mortgages and cash crankers to generate cash and cash flow for yourself. Chapter 13 will show you how to make money in many different areas of real estate.

You can also raise the rents for instant profit. Say a building is underrented by $50 per month per apartment. This is brought about by many factors in the marketplace. One factor is owner-managers living in the building. They get involved with tenants and don't keep up with the market rents.

How much could you raise the price of the building by raising the rent $50 per unit? Use a 10-unit building as an example, and say you could sell the building for 10 times gross. (This may vary in your area.) The value of the building would be gross rent times 10. To see how much $50 per month increases the value, just multiply:

Value increase = $50 per month × 12 months per year × 10 units × 10 times gross = $60,000

How long would it take you to increase the price in a building with month-to-month leases? One rental period, or 30 days. Just sent out a rental increase after you close. If you resold the building within a month or two after buying it, you would take your profit with almost no management problems.

LONG-TERM WEALTH BUILDING

In addition to the short-term areas of profit just covered, the later chapters in the book will also teach you how to build long-term profits (one year or longer). Long-term strategies include:

- *Equity Sharing*—Equity sharing will give you long-term management-free, problem-free profits. While you wait for appreciation to build wealth for you, your tenant-manager partner runs the property and takes care of it for you. See Chapter 9.
- *Lease-Options*—The option portion of a lease-option makes you long-term profit by letting you buy the property at a time when your price is below market and resell it at market value to generate cash and cash flow. The option is risk-free because if the profit is there, you exercise your option, and if it's not, you pass. See Chapter 10.
- *The Branches of the Tree*—Learn how to use rights of ownership to acquire property without using your cash. Sell down the road when the value has increased, and pay low taxes on your profits. See Chapter 12.
- *Learning to Use Dead Equities*—Learn how to control properties for future growth and profit by using the equity in raw land or properties you own right now.

WHAT'S GOING TO HAPPEN IN THE SHORT TERM?

The changes in real estate tax law will in the short term adversely affect the prices of commercial properties and apartment buildings, with the possible exception of small owner-managed apartments. (Tax shelter is still available to them.) Prices could drop as much as 10 to 15 percent. Rents should increase sharply over the next few years (due to loss of tax benefits), which should bring prices back up. User demand will remain strong for single-family homes, which should keep the prices up. Again, home ownership will be one of the last remaining tax shelters, because interest is still deductible on first and second homes.

If you see a drop of prices of apartment buildings over the next year or two, look at it as a buying opportunity. The new tax law will drive down construction of apartment buildings, which will create shortages and drive up rents. You can buy low and catch the rebound. Over the next few years (except for a real steal), I would hesitate to buy commercial property.

STRATEGY

Concentrate your investments into single-family homes over the short term. Pick homes that are easy to buy, say, ones with assumable FHA or VA loans and ones where the seller is willing to carry financing at a reasonable rate. In 1986 a lot of low-interest FHA and VA loans were created that will make good assumable loans. Limit your liability on loans, especially if you live in a state that permits deficiency judgments (if the property is sold for less than the value of the loans, they may sell other assets for satisfaction).

When the seller is carrying back financing, use an exculpatory clause to limit your liability. The clause might read something like, "The limit of liability of this mortgage shall be the property itself and shall not extend beyond it." Check with your attorney on wording. Protect yourself as much as possible.

Don't let changes in the tax law deter you from investing in real estate. It is still about the only hope of the average working man or woman to build wealth starting with little or nothing.

CHAPTER EIGHT

Ten Creative Ways to Generate a Down Payment

In some cases, with very motivated sellers, you can actually buy a property using none of your own cash. In most cases, however, the seller wants something. The mistake most investors make is to assume that that something has to be cash. Actually, many properties are bought by solving a seller's problem.

This chapter begins to train you to think of alternatives to cash. Think of these 10 techniques as a beginning, a foundation upon which to build a smorgasbord of ways to buy property without using your cash. If the seller is motivated, a transaction can generally be put together if you will stand back and say, "I know this can be put together; now what are some possible solutions?"

TEN BUILDING BLOCKS

When you exercise your muscles, they get stronger. When you exercise the creative parts of your brain, you will get better and easier solutions. Let's look at 10 building blocks. Feel free to expand.

The Time-Payment Down Payment

There are many cases where the seller doesn't need a down payment physically and yet won't sell for nothing down. Sellers feel or have heard that you should never sell a property without a down payment. Sometimes you can solve the problem just by giving the seller peace of mind. One suggestion, especially if a little extra payment is not a problem for you, is the installment down payment.

Here's an example: The seller wants a $3,000 down payment and a monthly payment of $700 per month. You suggest $800 per month for 30 months, and then $700 per month thereafter. How much is $100 extra per month for 30 months? $30 \times 100 = \$3,000$. That's the exact amount of the down payment the seller wanted.

Will this work every time? No. Should you suggest it? Yes. There are only two answers to the suggestion, and one of them is great. You buy property by suggesting solutions, not by assuming it can't be done.

Borrow the Down Payment

Don't start by assuming you can't borrow any money. Sit down and make a list; you need to look for alternatives. Have you purchased cash-value insurance? You can borrow that cash value from the insurance company at an incredibly low interest rate and use that for the down payment. If you're young, give your parents a call and see if they have any cash-value insurance. They could borrow the money at a low interest rate, lend it to you at, say, a 2 percent higher interest rate (which still gives you a great loan), and there's your down payment. As collateral, you could give them a second or third mortgage on the property you are buying. If you work at a large company, check and see if they have a credit union. You'll be amazed at how easy it is to borrow from your in-house credit union. They lend easily because they can have the monthly payment subtracted from your paycheck, which is a guaranteed repayment.

Seller's Equity as a Down Payment

If you use the seller's equity as the down payment, you are putting in no cash and your sole lender is the seller. This works when the seller is motivated, has a severe time limit, and must be divested of the property. The seller carries back a mortgage upon which you make monthly payments. The interest rate and monthly payment are both negotiable. (The more motivated the seller, the better the terms you will get.)

Take an example: A property is for sale at $100,000. The existing mortgage is an older FHA mortgage for $40,000, fully assumable. You take over the $40,000 mortgage, and the seller carries back a second mortgage in the amount of $60,000, terms to be agreed upon.

A friend of mine tells a cute story of his early investing days. He was approached by a woman who had found out he bought investment property. She had earlier purchased five FHA homes, applying for all the loans as owner-occupant. She said everything was going great until two FBI agents appeared at her door. The government had decided not to prosecute if she got rid of all the homes at no profit. Talk about motivated! My friend stepped in, took over all the loans, and got five properties for no down payment.

This is also an example of the rewards of advertising yourself as an investor. Advertising includes everything from running ads in the newspaper to ordering business cards that say you're an investor. (Pass them out generously.)

Assume Debt as a Down Payment

Many times the investor's so-called "need" for cash is a hidden need to pay off some other bills with the cash. Sometimes, as with the examples in Chapter 4, you can take over the debt in lieu of giving the seller cash to pay off the bills. If you have good credit and a little net worth, you may be welcome news to a banker who is having trouble getting payments from the seller of the property. It never hurts to ask.

Raise the Price/Lower the Terms

There is nothing wrong with appealing to a person's greed. Nothing gets a seller more excited than getting more for the property than he or she was orginally asking. This works well under the following conditions:

Condition 1: The seller wants $5,000 for a down payment, and you haven't been able to budge him off that amount. You only have $2,000, and you think the property is a great buy at the price he wants, or the property is in a neighborhood that is heating up and prices are starting to escalate (which means you can make a large profit in a short period just by controlling a piece of property). If the seller wants $100,000 with $5,000 down, you might offer $102,000 with $2,000 down. When you have held that property for years and it has doubled in value to $200,000, you won't care that you paid a little too much for it.

Condition 2: A property comes on the market, and it is obviously undervalued, say, an $80,000 house in a neighborhood of $100,000 homes. Offer a little more, say $82,000, for this reason: As soon as word gets around, a number of offers will hit the door, perhaps as many as four or five. Four of the offers will be for $80,000, and yours will be for $82,000. Give a little, and gain a lot.

Sweat Equity as a Down Payment

Using sweat equity as a down payment works especially well when the house obviously needs repairs and you are good with your hands. In the part of the offer where you put the down payment, you might write: "Buyer agrees to provide $3,000 in needed repairs to the property within 30 days of closing." If you can buy the materials for $300 or $400 and the rest of it is your labor, that's all the cash you have to provide to buy a house.

Skill for a Down Payment

Skill is a different down payment than sweat equity. If you have a skill that people are willing to pay money for, you can offer that skill as a down payment. You could be a plumber, carpenter, doctor, attorney, or whatever. It doesn't matter. You could offer so many hours of your time at so many dollars an hour (to be agreed upon), or you might, in the case of a doctor, offer one year's medical service to the family. Get creative, and write offers. You have nothing to lose. Stuck among all those "nos" you will find some "yeses."

Short-Term Note as a Down Payment

Many sellers who want all cash or a lot of cash for their property see little difference between cash at closing and cash three or four months after closing. It can mean a large difference to you. By having three or four months to raise the money, you can, under certain circumstances, do the whole thing with other people's money.

This works great with below-market rents. Rents are far from standard, even in a given neighborhood. While some owners are attentive and keep their rents at market, others are lazy or inattentive and let their rents fall below market. Owners who have lived in their buildings for years become emotionally involved with their tenants and tend to have below-market rents. Anytime you find below-market rents, there is an opportunity for profit.

For example, rents for apartments in a particular neighborhood are $400 per month. George, who has lived in his building for five years and values his tenants more than income, is charging only $300 per month. He has a total of 10 units. Say buildings in that area are selling for 9 times the gross income. How much can you raise the value of the building within 30 days after closing?

You could easily get $75 more per month for 10 units:

$75 per month × 10 units × 12 months × 9
(gross multiplier) = $81,000

Since you can raise the value of the building $81,000 with one 30-day notice of a rent raise, can you generate the cash to pay off a short-term note? In many cases, you can get a new loan based on a new appraisal with the new rents, pay off George's short-term note, and even put tax-free cash in your pocket (borrowed money isn't taxed).

Low rents and fixer-uppers (where the value of the property is raised quickly) are prime candidates for the short-term note.

Rents and Deposits as a Down Payment

With a little knowledge, you can greatly reduce the cash you must bring to a closing. Rents are paid in advance and must be refunded to a new buyer at time of closing. Deposits are the tenants' money, held by the owner, and must be passed to a new owner at time of sale.

Based on this knowledge, when is the best time to close a transaction if you are the buyer? How about the first or second of the month? Let's see what that means: Take a 10-unit building with rents of $400 per month. Say each tenant has a $200 deposit with the landlord. By closing on the first, you get in cash rebates of:

$$(\$400 \times 10 \text{ units}) + (\$200 \times 10 \text{ units}) = \$6,000$$

That's $6,000 less cash you have to bring to the closing. When you close *is* important.

Note: In some states, you must keep the deposits in a separate trust account, and you should, at all times, comply with the law. You would still, however, get credit for the rents.

The Blanket Mortgage as a Down Payment

A blanket mortgage (a mortgage on more than one property) makes a great down payment with a seller whose main objection is security. This seller doesn't need cash and would be willing to sell for no cash down, except for the worry that you might not pay him or her. After all, the seller says, with nothing in the property, you have nothing to lose.

Say you have a piece of land in Forever Estates. (They call it Forever Estates because it takes forever to sell the land.) You have almost or totally paid it off, and it's just sitting there. You say to the seller, "Mr. Seller, I want to prove to you I'm going to make the payments. For the equity you're going to lend me, I'm going to give you a blanket mortgage that covers not only your property, but my land also, so if you have to take back your property, you could also take my land."

Be sure to get a written release on your land after, say, one or two years (when you've proved yourself). You want this so the land will become available to satisfy the next security-conscious seller.

This arrangement gives you a use for an otherwise disappointing piece of land. Obviously, if you don't have such a property, your home or some other property would do nicely.

CHAPTER NINE

Equity Sharing: Make the Tenant Your Partner

Equity sharing literally means the sharing of equity. Since sharing indicates more than one, we know there must be at least two people involved. These two people, with totally different goals, can work together for their mutual benefit: the investor who wants hassle free profits, and the under-qualified renter who wants to become a homeowner.

Some people are touting equity sharing as the greatest thing since sliced bread. It's not. Had I equity-shared all of my earlier properties, I would have lost hundreds of thousands of dollars of profits. You can lose a lot of money equity sharing.

That doesn't mean you should never do it, but treat it for what it is. It's a problem-solving tool and nothing more. It solves two basic problems:

1. *Inability to Rent*—Even though you selected the property and the neighborhood with care, you've got a rental problem. The people who answered your ad

didn't check out well, and you're concerned about renting to them. Some time has gone by, and you either can't or don't want to carry the house any longer. Equity sharing can instantly fill the house up with a quality tenant.

2. *Negative Cash Flow*—Even though you've bought the property well using the techniques in this book, you couldn't wash it all out. You've still got $100 to $200 per month expenses above and beyond rent. You are either unable or don't want to carry it. Since equity sharing involves sharing the appreciation of the house with the tenant, you can ask the tenant to pay a little more than market rent.

For years, parents have done a form of equity sharing for their children. A lot of this tends to be more giving than sharing. The parents may have provided the down payment (and never been repaid), or they may assist with the monthly payment for a period of time until the children's income goes up. Modern versions have just put the situation on a businesslike basis, and equity sharing now may be between total strangers, each benefiting from the arrangement.

PROBLEMS IT SOLVES

To offset its lost profits, equity sharing does solve many problems. To the busy executive or the cautious investor, it may provide an avenue to real estate profits. Let's look at how equity sharing solves some problems.

Fear of Management

Many people voice concern about loss of sleep, which could affect their job. They've heard the story about the toilet overflowing at 2 A.M., and of the owner spending two or three hours getting the problem solved. Furthermore, nobody wants the mundane job of playing supply clerk, getting light bulbs and other service items supplied to a rental unit. With equity sharing, all minor problems and repairs are the responsibility of the tenant-owner.

Fear of Vacancies

If you're starting on a shoestring, you can run into trouble if you make two or three payments when you have no tenant. With equity sharing, there are no vacancies except for the rare occurrence of the tenant losing a job and not finding another. This will require getting a new tenant. You should quickly develop a waiting list from which to choose.

Fear of Collecting Rent

Many people don't invest in single-family homes because of the hassle of having to grind rent out of tenants every month. It's rough to make the payment out of your pocket while you're still trying to collect. (Proper screening can eliminate this.) With equity sharing, the tenant is an owner-partner who makes the payments because he or she is building an investment at the same time you are.

Fear of Damage

Everyone has heard horror stories of the tenant who trashed the house before leaving, so that truckloads of garbage had to be hauled away and the damage was in the thousands (another screening problem). You may have heard of a tenant tearing up a house, but have you ever heard of an owner tearing up a house? The tenant is a half-owner. You will find tenant-owners doing repairs, putting shelving in the garage, and doing other things that tend to raise the value of the property. Owners are like that.

Fear of Eviction

The thought of a tenant who doesn't pay rent and then refuses to move can turn some people away from ownership. With equity sharing, you'll be amazed at the quality of the tenants you can choose from. With people who value their reputations and have good credit to protect, the problems in this area can be minimal.

"Hammers Don't Fit My Hand, Golf Clubs Fit"

Some people—I'm one—have neither the talent for nor the interest in fixing up property. An unhandy person who fears large repair bills due to inability may decide not to invest in property. A tenant-owner-occupant to do all the minor repairs could give this investor the peace of mind he or she needs.

Fear of Negative Cash Flow

In some parts of the country today, negative cash flow is a true fear. With the market rents available, some investors see no way to avoid feeding the property. The knowledge that the tenant will willingly pay more than market rates can be enough to make property worth the investment.

WHAT ABOUT THE TENANTS?

Literally tens of thousands of people sincerely believe they can't buy a home. Some of these people have no down payment (and are firmly convinced they need one); others have business-created credit problems (and believe their credit must be perfect in order to buy a home). These multitudes are all candidates for a person who can put them into a home and show them how to build equity. How about you?

What attracts tenants to equity sharing?

No Down Payment

A young couple who desperately want a home but see no way to save up a down payment are good candidates for your program. If you took a survey of apartment dwellers and asked them for reasons why they weren't homeowners, first on the list, by far, would be lack of a down payment.

Tax Deductions

While it was not true five or ten years ago, more and more people are starting to stare mournfully at their paycheck stubs saying, "If I make $500 a week, how come I only get $360?" Using some fifth-grade math, you can show them how they can put extra money in their pocket, just by taking half of your house. (More on that later in this chapter.)

Appreciation

There are very few parts of this country where you can look at a consecutive five-year period and say, "Nothing much happened." When you plan your program over that long a period, your co-owners can be reasonably assured of making a nice profit at the end of your relationship.

Purchasing Power

Another candidate for equity sharing is a new arrival. Take Southern California, for instance. Thousands of people a year accept jobs from other areas of the country and move there. When a couple arrive from, say, the Midwest and start looking at home prices, all the blood drains out of their faces. They sold their lovely large home with acreage for $120,000 there, and they find they can buy a three-bedroom, two-bath crackerbox in an undesirable tract for the same money. They are faced with a difficult decision: live where they don't want to live (in the crackerbox) or, to get a better home, move so far away from work that commuting takes an hour or more. Neither option is very attractive.

You can have a solution for them, and make you both some money. If they have a block of cash, it's not even necessary that they put it into the house. If you provide the house (purchased for no down payment), they will be able to afford the payments by putting the cash into a money market fund, drawing interest, and taking out enough each month to make up the portion of the payment they can't afford to pay out of their salary. If you gave them the information about discounted mortgages, in Chapter 11, their cash may never run out.

Find prospects at main employers in your area. Put a simple typed note on the bulletin boards:

> INVESTOR WILL HELP YOU BUY A
> HOME. FOR DETAILS CALL HOLLIS,
> 888-9999.

Call and talk to the relocation officer in the company. After you convince him or her you plan to help the people, this person can be a valuable source of leads for new people coming into town. People who are good enough to be hired from a long distance away are pretty stable folks. They can make great co-owners.

OPPORTUNITIES ABOUND

From time to time certain cities become glutted with houses. These gluts occur mainly in one-industry areas. There may have been a boom, followed by a downward adjustment, which produces a larger glut. Or there may just have been a slump in the industry for a few years, producing a reduction of available jobs, which produced a glut of houses.

Although the opportunity to "steal" homes exists, the investor is faced with a major problem. The amateur investor truly doesn't know what to do. All of these available houses are competing for the available renters, and, following the laws of supply and demand, rents drop. Low rents, as they always do, create negative cash flow. This prevents unknowledgeable investors from making profits.

Equity sharing is a great solution. Even though there are few renters, they are in your properties, because you offer profits instead of a shoebox full of rent receipts. You can pull tenants out of existing rental houses with the lure of potential profits down the road.

Keep in mind you don't need to have a housing glut in order to make equity sharing work. You only need to find motivated sellers to buy from and a supply of people who want to become homeowners (they're in any city).

Finding Partners

To get a flood of prospective tenants, run this ad:

> I WILL DEED YOU HALF MY HOUSE IF
> YOU WILL MAKE THE PAYMENTS.
> HOLLIS, 888-9999.

Your phone should ring off the hook. You can not only pick the best tenant among many, you can develop a waiting list of co-owners, waiting for you to close another transaction.

Take a look at an equity-share situation. You have just bought the home shown in Figure 9A. You found very motivated sellers. They thought they had the home sold, but it fell out of escrow. In the meantime, they had bought their next home and are making payments on it. There was no way they could afford two payments, even for a few months, and they were extremely glad to get their price and get rid of the payment at the same time. You paid $80,000 for the house, took over an existing FHA loan with a payment of $625 per month for principal, interest, taxes, and insurance (PITI). The sellers were happy to carry back a $30,000

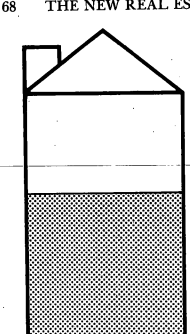

$80,000 House

$30,000 second mortgage:
10% interest-only—payable at
$250/month—due in 7 years

$50,000 FHA first mortgage:
12% interest at $625/month

Figure 9A

second mortgage with an interest-only payment of $250 per month, due in seven years. That gives you a total house payment of $875 per month. The problem is, the market rent in the neighborhood is only $725, leaving you with a negative cash flow of $150 per month. Although you can afford it, you want to buy at least 10 houses, and the thought of $1,500 per month could keep you awake nights.

So, you run the previous ad, and you get a nice couple, Jim and Jane Jones. You explain to them that they'll get half the house, and they will have to make the payment. Jim likes it, but he doesn't like having to pay $150 above market rent. You explain to him that he won't be paying it, the government will. Of their total payment of $875 per month, about $700 of it is interest and property tax, and both of these items are tax deductible. With a deduction of

$700 a month and being in a 28 percent tax bracket, they will get a tax refund amounting to $196 per month ($700 times .28).

Instead of losing $150 per month, they will make a profit of $46 per month just by taking your deal. Their rent money, instead of flushing down the drain, will come back to them at the time you settle, because of loan reduction (equity buildup) and appreciation. As a closer, you point out they can estimate their deduction, go down to their employer, reduce their withholding on their paycheck, and get this profit now. Jim and Jane are delighted, and you become partners.

How Do You Get Paid?

Since you don't want to be old and sitting on the front porch of a home waiting for Jim and Jane to sell their home so you can take your profits, set a time limit on the agreement. I suggest five years, since a shorter period of time may not be sufficient for the home to go up enough in value. At only a 5 percent appreciation rate compounded, the home would be worth about $107,000 after five years. Even after selling costs, you would have at least $20,000 to split. Over a five-year period, it's rare if there isn't a surge in values, which could give you a lot more than that amount to split.

What if they want to stay in the home? Work with them. Of course, if they stayed, there would be no selling costs, and you would split, in the above example, $27,000. You could take your $13,500 (half) as part cash, and carry back a mortgage at a good interest rate for the balance.

If you put eight or ten of these together, and the paydays start to arrive, you could find the need to work for a wage rapidly disappearing. If you set it up so several matured each year (like certificates of deposit), you could eliminate all need to work for a wage.

INVESTOR-INVESTOR EQUITY SHARING

To make investor-investor equity sharing work effectively, some conditions must exist. You must buy a property at healthy discount from a motivated seller. The seller will have severe financial problems or a problem that seems unsolvable to him or her.

By the way, you can make a lot of money in this world by solving "unsolvable" problems. Look at Figure 9B.

As shown in the illustration, you have a property with a $200,000 value. It has an assumable $100,000 first mortgage with a $25,000 second mortgage due in 60 days.

The seller has a problem. Because of business setbacks, he is cash-poor, and his credit report has been damaged. He is one payment behind on his second mortgage and believes

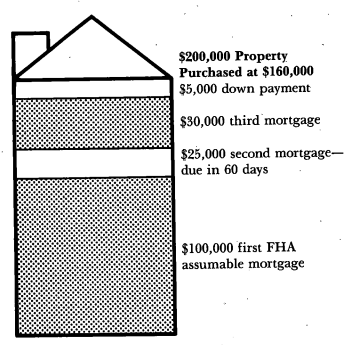

**$200,000 Property
Purchased at $160,000**
$5,000 down payment

$30,000 third mortgage

$25,000 second mortgage—
due in 60 days

$100,000 first FHA
assumable mortgage

Figure 9B

that he is not in a position to borrow money. Having received a letter from the holder of the second mortgage demanding payment and threatening foreclosure, he has visions of losing all of his equity in the property.

You make the following offer:

$ 5,000	Down Payment (can be in the form of a note due in 60 days)
100,000	First Mortgage to Be Assumed
25,000	Second Mortgage to Be Assumed (due in 60 days)
30,000	Third Mortgage to Be Carried by Seller
$160,000	Total Price

Basically, you are offering to clear up the problem of the second mortgage and to give the seller a $30,000 mortgage for his equity upon which you will make payments.

To accomplish this you sell half of the property to an investor for $40,000 in cash. You take $25,000 and pay off the second mortgage, which would move your mortgage to second position. You take $5,000 and give it to the seller for his down payment, and you take the remaining $10,000 and put it in your pocket.

Now, what do you have? Figure 9C on page 72 illustrates the answer.

What's in it for the investor? She has put in $40,000 cash, and she has one-half interest in a building that has a built-in $70,000 in equity, half of which is hers ($35,000 worth). She gets half of all the tax benefits, and she shares in half of all the profit from any appreciation. Could you do all this in one closing? Of course you could. Make your offer subject to partner's approval, and present it to the investor. Put in her cash (the $40,000), pay off everybody as previously described, and walk away from the closing with $10,000 cash in your pocket and a half interest in the building. All you really did was package.

How can you motivate your partner more? Change the

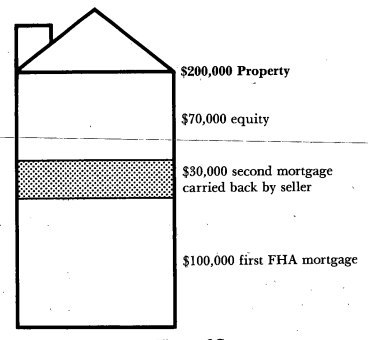

$200,000 Property

$70,000 equity

$30,000 second mortgage
carried back by seller

$100,000 first FHA mortgage

Figure 9C

percentage of ownership. Offer the investor 60 percent of ownership. How about 70 percent? Your profit would still be substantial. You might offer to do the lion's share of the management. Leave the investor some to qualify for the depreciation deduction.

THE EQUITY-SHARING AGREEMENT

The Internal Revenue Code requires that equity sharing between resident and nonresident co-owners be done by written agreement (IRC §280A). Any agreement between the two parties should be prepared by a *real estate* attorney. You can also get equity-sharing agreements as well as mortgage financing by contacting the Family Backed Mortgage Association. Call 1-800-323-3262 or, in California, 1-

800-232-3262. Their fee, at the time of this writing, is $250.

Some basics that a good equity-sharing agreement should have include:

1. The details of a buyout agreement between the parties—Either party should be able to buy the other out using terms agreed upon in the original agreement.
2. A procedure for settling any disputes—Attorneys and courts are very expensive. Arbitration is usually a better solution.
3. A rental agreement where the nonresident-owner agrees to rent his or her portion of the home to the resident-owner—The portion of the rent paid should be based on fair market rent. There should be some kind of provision for rent raises as a function of time (perhaps yearly).
4. The percentages of ownership of both parties—It doesn't always have to be 50/50.
5. The maximum time available for dividing the proceeds (through sale, refinance, or the creation of a mortgage)—To allow for reasonable appreciation, the time period should be five years or longer.
6. How the profit is split upon sale of the house—Any initial cash investment by the nonresident-owner should be returned before any profits are split.
7. How maintenance costs are to be handled—The agreement should spell out the difference between minor costs (below some dollar amount) and major costs (replacement of a roof). Who pays for what?

A FAMILY EQUITY-SHARE

Fred Jr., recently married, wanted a home for himself and his new bride. Although his income is good, his current bank balance is near zero. He approaches Fred Sr., his father, and they come the following agreement:

Purchase:	$100,000 home
Down payment:	$20,000 provided by Fred Sr.
Balance:	$80,000 loan at 11 percent for 30 years payable at $761.86 per month
Ownership:	Fred Jr. and wife, ½ owners Fred Sr., ½ owner
Payments made:	$380.96 paid by Fred Jr.
	$380.96 paid by Fred Sr.
	$400 paid by Fred Jr. to Fred Sr. for rent of ½ of the house
Profit split:	$20,000 returned to Fred Sr. after 10 years, and balance split 50/50 between the two parties
Benefits:	Fred Sr.—
	Gets tax benefits of ½ of house through depreciation (if qualified under the management provision of the new tax code)
	Writes ½ of property tax off on his income tax
	Gets ½ of equity buildup (principal portion of the $380.96 monthly payment)
	Helps son and daughter-in-law buy a home
	Gets ½ of appreciation
	Has positive cash flow of $19.04 per month ($400 rent minus $380.96 payment). When you throw in the tax shelter, which generates a

	return of tax dollars, the positive cash flow is much higher.
Benefits:	Fred Jr.—
	Gets home to live in now
	Gets ½ of the monthly interest plus ½ of the property tax as an income tax deduction. This also reduces his monthly outlay by returning tax dollars.
	Gets ½ of equity buildup
	Gets ½ of appreciation

This chapter is only a taste. There are many more exciting ways to put transactions together. As you go to work in real estate, ideas will occur to you that haven't to me. When you put one together, write to me in care of the publisher, and I will share with other investors in future books. We will learn together.

CHAPTER TEN

Lease-Options: Lower the Risk and Raise the Profit

The lease-option is two distinct things. A *lease* merely allows the quiet use of a property in return for a payment, usually cash and usually monthly. If you can lease a property for below market (what someone else will pay for it), you can develop a monthly cash flow. The *option* is a right to buy something at a predetermined ‚price and a predetermined time.

You don't have to own a piece of real estate in order to make a profit, you only have to control it. A lease with option to buy is a beautiful controlling vehicle.

WHERE TO FIND LEASE-OPTIONS

One source of lease-options is the Real Estate for Sale column in your local newspaper's classified ads. The average would-be seller is not that interested in a lease-option. The motivated seller, who is looking for any way out, can sometimes be talked into it. When doing your normal weekly calling from the ads, you might add the question, "Would you consider a lease-option?" Where other financing doesn't work, it may be possible to buy a house using a lease-option. It's another avenue to explore.

The greatest place to find a lease-option situation is in the Houses for Rent column. Everybody in that column has a problem. They have a vacant house, and they have to dig down in their pocket every month and make a payment with no help in sight. In fact, every 15 or so ads, you will see the word *option*.

Other owners, looking to see if their ad has been placed, see the word *option* in other ads. Many of those who don't mention it would consider it, if only asked.

Let's look at some types of owners in the column.

1. Sam tried to sell his house and had no luck. After a while he listed it with an agent who, through ineptness or a sluggish market, didn't sell it. A few people came through, but nobody wrote an offer. The listing expired. Sam, tired of making the payments (he's moved to another home), is now trying to rent the house. He's open to about anything.
2. Bill is much better off. He's making a lot of money and needs the house for tax shelter. He'll be ready to sell in three more years after he depreciates the house for that period. A lease followed by a sale would be perfect for him.
3. When you ask, you learn that Alice hadn't thought about it before. You bring up the benefits to her: (1) No vacancies—you get a tenant who is going to stay there for the agreed-upon period. (2) Quality tenants—even if the option isn't taken, you always get a better tenant and better treatment of the house when the tenant is a potential owner. Alice may or may not go for it, but there are only two answers, and one of them is great. If she indicates even a mild interest, leave your phone

number. You may get a phone call later, if the place doesn't rent, and it costs you nothing.

If there's no interest whatsoever, thank the person you call for his or her time and call the next number. You've got better things to do with your time than to try to talk people into it.

An excellent trial question to ask is, "If I gave you a two-year lease, would you give me an option to buy?" The thought of two years with no tenant problems (especially if they've had them) could be enough to make a lease-option seem worth a try.

THE MOST CRITICAL CLAUSE

The most critical clause in your contract is a right to sublet. You want to put a tenant into the place and use the tenant's money to make your profit.

Some owners will not want to give you a right-to-sublet clause, but you must insist. You might say, "Mr. Seller, I'm agreeing to pay this money for several years; what happens if my company moves me or I lose my job? I've got to have the right to put someone else in. I can't afford two house payments. I've got to plan my life."

Be quiet, and let the seller talk; you could get an agreement. If the seller insists on the right to approve the tenant, you should insist that the contract say that consent is "not to be unreasonably withheld."

CONSIDERATION

Most owners want some cash consideration in front in exchange for giving you an option, perhaps as much as several thousand dollars. Few of us would like to pay it. If you're starting cash-poor, you *can't* pay it. Fortunately, not many motivated sellers insist on it. If you limit yourself to the very motivated (see earlier chapters), you can avoid putting down cash for options. Let's take a look at some examples.

SOLVING AN UNREASONABLE PROBLEM

This story refers to the next diagram, Figure 10A. A well-heeled business executive from the Northwest came out to the Sun Belt for a well-deserved rest. Having left in the wintertime, he noticed something very nice when he arrived: He wasn't freezing. He thought, "What a wonderful place this would be to retire. Even though I won't retire for 10 years, why not buy a house now, rent it out when I can, and use it sometimes in the winter months?" Not knowing the area, and wanting to enjoy his vacation, he quickly found a house for sale for $78,000 with an assumable FHA loan with PITI payments of $450 per month. Liking the hassle-free purchase, he paid cash to the loan and closed quickly.

He found out later he had overpaid for the house; it was worth only $70,000. Returning home, and getting tied up in his business, he really had second thoughts. The whole idea had soured for him, and he just wanted out. He decided to sell the house.

Look at his problem. If he sells the house in a conventional manner, what happens to him? The first thing he has to do is lower the price $8,000 to bring it down to market so it will sell. Then he has to sell it. From that far away, he's got real estate commission, closing costs, and attorney's fees—perhaps as much as $7,000. He stands to lose as much as $15,000 just getting rid of the house. That's certainly not very attractive to the seller.

Along comes an investor. She offers $400 a month on a lease, with an option to buy the property after four years for $78,000, the price the seller wants. The executive thinks, "If I take this offer, I don't have to lose $15,000 anymore." The only problem he has is with the negative cash flow. (He would pay out $450 on the loan, and the investor would pay

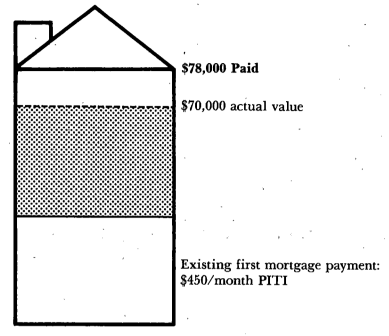

$78,000 Paid

$70,000 actual value

Existing first mortgage payment:
$450/month PITI

Figure 10A

him $400 per month.) The investor points out that the
minus $50 per month can be used as a tax write-off to offset
income from his other real estate investments, and at the
same time he gets rid of his problem (the house). The seller
accepts.

Let's see what happens to this investor. She knows she
can rent the house easily for $475 per month. Since she is
paying $400 per month, her positive cash flow is $75 per
month. The first year she takes in $900 in cash. In year 2 she
raises the rent $50 per month, and her positive cash flow
goes to $125 per month. That year she takes in $1,500 in
positive cash flow. The third year she raises the rent
another $50, and her positive cash flow goes to $175 per
month ($125 + $50). Her positive cash flow that year is
$2,100. In the fourth and last year, she raises her rent

another $50, and her positive cash flow goes to $225 per month ($175 + $50). Her positive cash flow that year is $2,700. As shown in Table 10A, her total positive cash flow for the four years is $7,200.

First Year	Second Year	Third Year	Fourth Year
$75/month positive cash flow: $900 1st year	$125/month positive cash flow: $1,500 2nd year	$175/month positive cash flow: $2,100 3rd year	$225/month positive cash flow: $2,700 4th year

Total cash flow = $900 + $1,500 + $2,100 + $2,700 = $7,200

Table 10A

Now the lease expires and it's option time. Should the investor buy the house? Remember, it's her option, not the seller's. Did the house appreciate? Is it worth more than $78,000? If so, she should buy it and take the extra profit. Is it worth less than $78,000? She should walk away, and keep the $7,200 she made in positive cash flow. Notice that the investor makes money if the house appreciates, and she makes money if the house never appreciates. If the market-place takes off and prices shoot up, she has the opportunity to make $10,000 or $15,000 more. Learning to package lease-options can be a profitable venture.

SOLVING A SELLER'S PROBLEM

An investor found a house worth $75,000 with an exist-ing FHA loan of $40,000 with a PITI payment of $425. He started to negotiate with the seller and found the seller didn't want to sell. The seller's tax advisor had told her to hold the house for three more years (to use the depreciation) before she sold it, subject to the limitations under the new tax law.

It was a good property in a good neighborhood, so the

investor switched his tack to a lease-option. He said, "Why not arrange your sale now, eliminate any management headaches, keep the tax benefits, and make your CPA happy?" He made the following proposal:

Lease for 3 years:	*Purchase:*	
$550 per month	$85,000	price
	$ 5,000	down payment
	$40,000	first mortgage assumed
	$40,000	second mortgage carried by seller—5 years, 10% interest only

The seller accepted. The investor has an agreed-upon lease, plus firm price and terms for the purchase (very critical). Where will the $5,000 down payment come from? The investor asked for, and got, the stipulation that $125 on the lease payment would apply to the down payment:

$$\$125 \times 12 \text{ months} \times 3 \text{ years} = \$4,500$$

The investor was confident he could come up with $500. Although the property was currently rented for $500 per month, the investor knew rents in the area and was firmly convinced the current rent was low. He knew he could get $575. He also felt the area was heating up and the rent could be raised during the three-year lease period.

Will he make money on appreciation? Five percent appreciation compounded would make the house worth about $87,000 in three years. In a hot area, he could possibly get more appreciation. Remember, if nothing happens, he can walk away and keep any positive cash flow. The option belongs to him, not the seller.

BUYING THE HIGH-PRICED SPREAD

Do you have a section of your city with expensive homes? Did you know there are people in those areas who are having a hard time selling their homes? People are not buying them for rentals because they don't make any sense that way. You might have a $200,000 house which, if purchased, would require a $2,000 a month payment that rents for only $1,200. Who wants to feed it $800 a month?

If that house had been purchased, for instance, 10 years ago for $100,000, has doubled in value, and has an existing payment of around $1,000 or a little more (the original payment when the house was new), it is a prime candidate for a lease-option. You could get cash flow on the difference between the $1,200 rent and the $1,000 payment. Also, you might end up making, on a home that expensive, $30,000 or $40,000 on appreciation. It's sure worth a few hours of your time working on it. How much an hour would you be paying yourself?

A SANDWICH LEASE

A sandwich lease is a lease of a lease. This could be a case where you took a lease-option at a below-the-market rent lease payment and then gave a lease-option based on your lease-option at a higher monthly lease payment. You would have the due date on the option you give come due before yours expires. You could then take the cash you received and use it to exercise your option. Any monthly payment your lessee makes that is higher than yours is profit to you. Any amount the optionee pays for the house that is higher than the amount you're paying (at option time) is profit for you. Remember, the more motivated the seller, the better lease payment and option price you can get. It's food for thought.

ANOTHER WAY TO USE AN OPTION

I read of a woman who was going to state tax sales. What's sold is property that has been taken back for nonpayment of taxes. This woman said she went to land sales. While there was a lot of competition at the sales of improved property, almost no one was at the land sales. She picked up two lots valued at $30,000 each at a well-known Southern California resort for $3,000 each. A couple had gotten divorced, left the state in separate directions, and just abandoned the land. She bought it for 10 cents on the dollar.

What if you found a million-dollar piece of land in an area of the state that is heating up, and yet its availability wasn't total public knowledge? Perhaps the owner lived out of state and would jump at the chance to sell for a price greater than what he originally paid. You could offer an option to buy that land for $1 million, valid for 18 months. The option fee would be the $30,000 piece of land you paid $3,000 for. If, in the heating-up area, you picked up 10 percent appreciation, that's $100,000. Your $3,000 cash is at risk; if you lose it, the loss is tax-deductible. This technique is useful for land that has value but is not very salable.

LEASE-OPTION A FIXER-UPPER

Figure 10B shows financing for a rundown house in a good neighborhood (the worst house on the best block). The current price it would sell for would be $60,000; however, if a few thousand dollars were spent on it, it would sell for $70,000. Its poor appearance makes selling difficult, and the owner has neither the money nor the desire to fix it up. It has an existing FHA loan with PITI payments of $250 per month. Current market rent would be $500 per month, if it were in good condition.

You lease for $350 per month with an option to buy in four years for $70,000. You prime the seller's pump by pointing out she will get $100 a month while she waits, and $10,000 more for the property by taking your offer. She also agrees to give you $50 a month credit toward the down payment.

You fix it up and lease it for $500 per month, which more than covers your $350 payments. The first year, you make $150 per month, for a total of $1,800. The second year, you

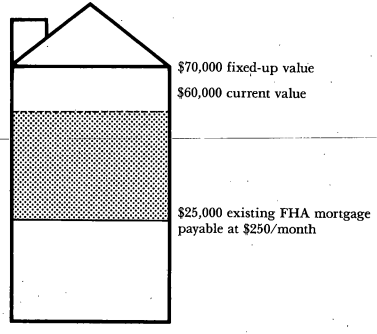

$70,000 fixed-up value

$60,000 current value

$25,000 existing FHA mortgage payable at $250/month

Figure 10B

raise the rent $50 and make $200 per month ($2,400 per year). With another raise, you make $250 per month the third year ($3,000 total). The fourth year, you make $300 per month ($3,600 per year). The total for the four years is:

$1,800 + $2,400 + $3,000 + $3,600 = $10,800

You also are saving money toward the down payment. The seller credits you $50 a month. For 48 months, that's $2,400 applied to the down payment.

Say the property appreciates to $100,000 in 3 to 5 years. You refinance with a new $80,000 loan. Put around $15,000 cash into your pocket (the difference between the new loan and the old loan), pay no income tax until you sell, and you still have $20,000 in equity.

CHAPTER ELEVEN

Mortgage Discount Techniques: The Wealth of Our Times

To understand why mortgages are discounted, you must understand the time value of money. Let's take an example: Which would you rather have, $10,000 now, or $10,000 a year from now? Funny thing, 100 people out of 100 say, "I'll take it now." Money now is better than money later.

What if, for some reason, you want some cash now or, even worse, you have to have some cash now? You come to me and say, "Hollis, I've got $10,000 coming in one year, and I need some cash. Why don't you give me the $10,000, and I'll give it back to you in one year?" Well, what's in it for me? I would turn you down. If you said, "Give me $9,000 now, and I'll give you $10,000 a year from now," I still might turn you down, but what you are saying is starting to make sense. If you said, "Give me $8,000 now, and I'll give you $10,000 a year from now," you would be getting my attention.

Money has a time value, and bankers have been getting rich on that knowledge for centuries. If you could borrow money at 12 percent and rent it out at 20 percent, could you make a profit? Ask any banker.

PRINCIPLES OF DISCOUNTING

If you are going to understand why people would sell a mortgage at discount, you must understand that lives are not static. Goals change, needs change, desires change, and people just change their minds. Here's a story to help you understand: George had been trying to sell his boat for quite some time in a depressed boat market. He had run ads and more ads, and he was beginning to wonder if anybody would buy it. He had been asking $2,000, but he was considering dropping the price to $1,500 just to get rid of it.

The next day Jim arrived. George could tell Jim liked the boat. Finally Jim said, "Let's load it on my truck." George, having had some sales training, recognized a buying signal when he heard one. He jumped to help Jim load the boat. When the boat was about half on, Jim said, "There is one small problem. I don't have $2,000 although I'm willing to pay that for this boat." George, who had already considered the boat sold, slumped. Jim continued, "The good news is, I will have money in two months. I need the boat in my business now, and I will give you a 60-day note for the money and pay you then." George thought for a moment, realized he was getting top dollar and there were no other buyers in sight, and decided to accept.

A month goes by, and everything is fine. George's brother comes over, and George has never seen him more excited. He starts to tell George about a business opportunity, and the more he talks, the more excited George becomes. He is convinced a fortune can be made, and his brother wants him for a partner. The brother then says, "The good news is we only have to put up $1,000 each." George, still wanting it badly, says, "I don't have any cash, but Jim owes me some money. Let me call him." He calls Jim and asks for the money. Jim explains he won't have it for another three or four weeks, and he will pay at that time. George's brother says, "If we don't have the money in three days, we'll lose the deal."

George is heartbroken. Contacting his local banker, he finds out they don't want to lend on a personal note. George, feeling all is lost, is telling his sad story to a friend. The friend, who happens to know Jim and thinks he will pay, says to George, "I'll buy Jim's note, and I'll give you $1,000 for it." George, being a shrewd negotiator, shouts, "I'll take it!"

Who's the loser here? Nobody. George got the business he wanted, and the friend got 100 percent return on his money in one month ($2,000 back on the note he paid $1,000 for), which made him very happy. There doesn't have to be a loser in these transactions. It depends on what's going to be done with the money.

USE A DISCOUNT FOR A DOWN PAYMENT

The discounting principle gives you a way to work with an unmotivated seller. Take a look at Figure 11A. A $100,000 piece of property for sale has two mortgages, a first mortgage, held by Mr. and Mrs. Jones, and a second mortgage, held by Mr. and Mrs. Frump.

The seller is definitely not motivated. He wants his price, and he wants all cash. You might be wondering why you're even trying to buy it. Well, wait a minute. The property is a good buy, is in a great neighborhood, and has a lot of potential profit, so don't give up yet. If the seller isn't flexible, perhaps the mortgage holders are.

Let's look at their situations: The Joneses, a happily married middle-aged couple, own the first mortgage. They have carried it back for a good number of years since they sold the property, and they were just going to live on the income. However, in the five years they have owned it, prices have gone up, and they are starting to believe they

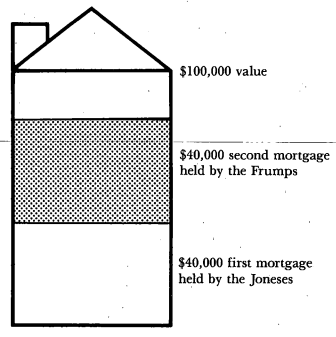

$100,000 value

$40,000 second mortgage
held by the Frumps

$40,000 first mortgage
held by the Joneses

Figure 11A

might be able to buy only a loaf of bread with their last
payment. They're convinced they're going to have to start
investing in order to survive financially. You call them up
and say, "Would you take $30,000 in cash for your mort-
gage?" They happily accept.

The Frumps are a different story. Fred Frump and Frieda
Frump are having their problems. They think a day with
only four or five bad arguments is a good one. Frieda
finally says to Fred, "You no-good, lazy, good-for-nothing
lousy excuse for a man, I'm not going to take this anymore.
I want out of this marriage. You give me $30,000 in cash,
and I'm history." This sounds like it's heaven-sent to Fred;
the only problem is, he doesn't have the cash. You call up
and say, "Would you take $30,000 cash for your mortgage?"
Fred, kissing the phone because he knows you can't see
him, says, "Well, I'd certainly consider it."

Now you have two $40,000 mortgages you can buy for $30,000 each. The only problem is, you don't have the $60,000. Who does? The friendly officer at the savings and loan association, and she makes a living making real estate loans. You write up a sales contract to buy the $100,000 property with the S&L providing a new $80,000 mortgage, and you will put $20,000 down. On the loan application form you will find a question that asks, "What is the source of your down payment?" You reply, "In escrow." The purchase price is $100,000, and when the S&L funds the $80,000 mortgage, the transaction will close. Is the down payment in escrow? Of course it is. It's the discount. The transaction closes, and you have a $100,000 piece of property in which you have $20,000 worth of equity, and yet you bought it with none of your cash.

THE CASH AND EQUITY CRANK

Look at Figure 11B. Here is an excellent property to use the discounting technique with. You have a $120,000 house with a $90,000 private mortgage, a 20-year seller carryback at 11 percent with 15 years left to run. Again, the mortgagees are a couple whose investment concept has changed. They are convinced that runaway deficits have to bring runaway inflation, it's just a matter of time (a position you would be derelict in your duty not to point out to them). They are aware (or you point out to them) that longer-term mortgages take a deeper discount. The cash value of this mortgage is only about $50,000. The other advantage you have is that the seller wants only $10,000 as a down payment.

Write an offer: purchase price, $120,000; down payment, $10,000; buyer to get a $20,000 second mortgage from the seller and a new $90,000 first mortgage. The three of these items add up to $120,000. Where's your down payment for the lender? Why, in escrow, of course. Let's see what everybody brings to the escrow.

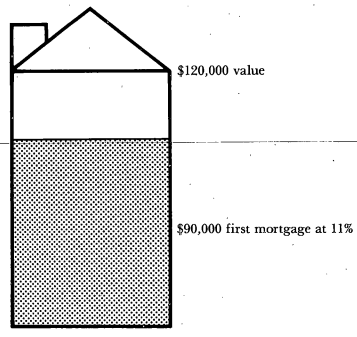

$120,000 value

$90,000 first mortgage at 11%

Figure 11B

Look at the escrow diagram, Figure 11C. In escrow is $90,000 in cash, of which you have to pay $50,000 to the holders of the original private note and $10,000 to the seller for a down payment (payout total is $60,000). The new financing on the house (a total of $110,000) will give you a $10,000 equity in the property. So, you walk out of the escrow with $30,000 in cash and $10,000 in equity. Not a bad day's work. What if the lender says, "I want more down payment before I'll fund this loan"? You can afford it. Also, closing costs are involved.

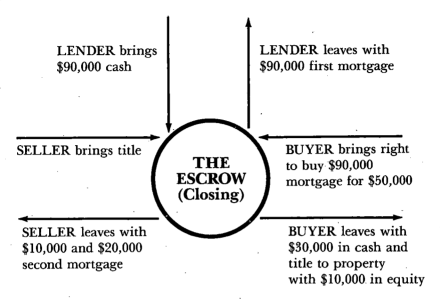

LENDER brings
$90,000 cash

LENDER leaves with
$90,000 first mortgage

SELLER brings title

THE ESCROW (Closing)

BUYER brings right
to buy $90,000
mortgage for $50,000

SELLER leaves with
$10,000 and $20,000
second mortgage

BUYER leaves with
$30,000 in cash and
title to property
with $10,000 in equity

Figure 11C

IF YOU KEEP ON FISHING, YOU CAN HOOK A BIG ONE

An astute discounter discovered a situation with a lot of potential profit. He found a group who had a $3 million mortgage on a $5 million property. They had a pressing need to invest $2 million in a business venture, and they were willing to sell the mortgage for that amount. The investor told them he would get back to them in a few days because he didn't have the money. Since the mortgage paid a respectable 13½ percent, he thought he knew who did.

He started calling bankers. What he was looking for was a banker with a serious problem he could solve. He found one with a $700,000 piece of land he had taken back from a builder and, because of other money advanced to try to save the situation, he was owed a total of $800,000. He knew that to sell the land for cash he would have to discount the value, and he was in trouble. Sitting down with the banker, our investor suggested some mutual back scratching. He said, "Mr. Banker, I've got a friend with a $3 million mortgage that pays 11 percent on a $5 million building. If your trust department will buy that note, I will give you $800,000 cash for your $700,000 piece of land." If you want to get a banker's attention, solve a difficult problem for him or her. The banker went to talk to his trust department and, subject to verification, they agreed.

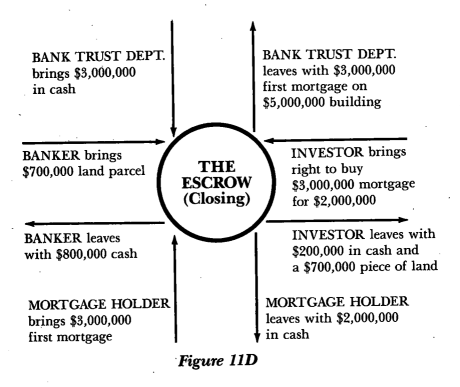

BANK TRUST DEPT.
brings $3,000,000
in cash

BANK TRUST DEPT.
leaves with $3,000,000
first mortgage on
$5,000,000 building

BANKER brings
$700,000 land parcel

THE ESCROW (Closing)

INVESTOR brings
right to buy
$3,000,000 mortgage
for $2,000,000

BANKER leaves
with $800,000 cash

INVESTOR leaves with
$200,000 in cash and
a $700,000 piece of land

MORTGAGE HOLDER
brings $3,000,000
first mortgage

MORTGAGE HOLDER
leaves with $2,000,000
in cash

Figure 11D

Figure 11D shows the escrow. In the escrow are $3 million in cash, a $700,000 piece of land, and a $3 million mortgage. What happens to the cash? Well, $2 million of it goes to the owner of the mortgage, and $800,000 of it goes to the banker, leaving $200,000. The mortgage goes to the trust department of the bank. What's left? There is $200,000 in cash, but there is also a $700,000 free-and-clear, buildable piece of land. Who gets all that? The escrow agent had to give it to the investor, because everybody else had gone home. A $900,000 profit. The investor's profit was the discount of $1 million less the $100,000 he had to "overpay" for the land. As the miner said, "There's gold in them thar hills."

These situations don't grow on trees or fall into your lap. They are far from a piece of cake. They are, in fact, a lot of hard work. You can work for a month or two on one transaction, have it fall apart, and get nothing. That doesn't mean you should avoid this area. If you're an investor already, spend a little time working on mortgages. If you're a beginner, don't work on this and nothing else. It's not that you won't put a transaction together, it's just that you might become discouraged before any money actually comes. If you're putting in ten hours per week, put in two on discounted mortgages and eight on the other investment ideas in this book. Sooner or later, you will pop one.

THE WORLD OF DISCOUNTED MORTGAGES

Now you'll encounter a world you might not have known existed: the marketplace of discounted paper. Billions of dollars change hands every year, and hundreds of millions of dollars of profits are reaped by knowledgeable investors who work this marketplace. It's difficult to cover in a single chapter (or even in a book) the many ways you can turn a profit. What this discussion will give you is some ideas. These are meant to be building blocks that you can use to expand your knowledge and have this world open up to you.

First let's take a look at the commercial marketplace. You only have to pick up your local newspaper, unless you live in a very small town, and turn to the classified ads. In the

real estate section, you will find buyers and sellers of real
estate mortgages or trust deeds (depending on your state—
some states have both). Under buyers, you might see ads
like:

Cash for your mortgage
Jones Mortgage Co.
333-6666

Or you might see one like:

Fair prices paid for 1st and 2nd TDs
Joe 444-5555

The difference is that one ad is for a commercial business
and the other is for a private buyer of mortgages (known in
the trade as paper). A typical seller's ad might read:

2nd TD avail on prime Westsd resid. LTV
80% $101,500 due in 7 yrs. 11-3/4% int.
pay $600 mo. $88,000 agt. 222-4444

Ad copy is expensive, so advertisers abbreviate a lot. In
English that ad said: A second trust deed is available on a
prime westside residence. The loan-to-value ratio is 80
percent. In other words, there is 20 percent equity in the
property, above and beyond the mortgage, to protect the
investment. The loan is due in 7 years and carries an
interest rate of 11¾ percent. The payment is $600 per month,
and they will sell the trust deed for $88,000. As you will
learn later in this chapter, this is *not* the buy of a lifetime.
It is merely used as an example. In a recent copy of the
Sunday *Los Angeles Times,* I counted 28 sellers and 30
buyers of trust deeds.

WHERE TO FIND MORTGAGES

The newspaper is not the place where you're going to
find any real bargains; the competition is too fierce. If you
work this section, take the suggestion in Chapter 3. Get the
Sunday paper on Saturday, then go through it and work any

bargain you will find on Saturday afternoon or evening before the whole world starts to call on Sunday. Get the purchase tied up in writing, if you can.

Following are some suggestions for better places to find mortgages.

Mortgage Brokers

Mortgage brokers are people who deal with mortgages for a living. They arrange loans, and they also sell mortgages at a discount. States vary in their requirements for licensing to be an agent for mortgages. To be a broker, you may need a special license, need a real estate license, be bondable, or none of these. Fortunately for the consumer, few states have no requirements at all.

To find mortgage brokers, look in the Yellow Pages. Spend a little time. These people get several phone calls a week from people saying they want to buy mortgages, and most of them don't pan out. Make an appointment and go in and see them personally. Let them know you're serious. Tell them what you're looking for, and ask them to call you when they find it.

If you make the requirements too tough, you won't get many phone calls. Or the broker may tell you that if a mortgage that good turns up, he or she will buy it personally. Too much greed will produce no profit, so be reasonable. By taking a look at what the broker has for sale, you will get an idea of what mortgages are selling for in your area.

Realtors

Real estate brokers and Realtors are a good source of potential buys. They have clients who have expressed a need for cash in exchange for their mortgages, and they may even have listings. You might suggest, "Why don't you contact the mortgage holders on property you sold a year ago or longer, and see if they would like to have cash for their mortgage? It's possible we can both make some money." If they're in a slow period, they could get excited about the prospect.

Exchangers

Exchangers are agents who specialize in tax-free exchanges of real estate. There aren't many exchanges around that are free of a need for cash. In times when new mortgages are expensive, it is possible that discounting a mortgage for cash can be the difference between the transaction working and not working.

Let exchangers know you're in the market. How do you find them? Again, the tried-and-true Yellow Pages.

Bankruptcy Trustees

Most people go into bankruptcy for one reason: a shortage of cash. Whether it is liquidation (see Chapter 8) or a reorganization (see Chapter 12), it is quite possible they need cash to solve the problem. If there is an existing mortgage, it is quite possible you can buy it at a nice discount. Contact your local courthouse and find out the names of some trustees. Write them a letter, telling them you're a buyer. You can, in some cases, pick up a real bargain.

The County Courthouse

All mortgages are recorded. These are public records, available to you. Out-of-state mortgage holders are especially attractive. They have to be a little nervous, holding a mortgage on a property in a state where they no longer reside. Write to them and see if they have an interest in selling. If so, get the details and write them an offer. The nice thing here is that you'll have no competition. Your offer will probably be the only offer. This is a lot of work, but you can get some good buys.

Attorneys

Any attorney involved in probating wills can be a great source of mortgages available for discount. What do estates need? Cash. It's needed both to settle the estate and to pay estate taxes. (The IRS is not noted for its patience.) Contact them by phone, tell them what you are looking for, and then follow it up with a letter they can put in their files. (Phone numbers written on scratch paper are seldom called.)

CPAs

Anyone who does taxes will have clients who need cash to pay income tax. Again, phone calls plus a letter will work. If you live in a big city, limit your work to the area in which you live. Otherwise, there are just too many attorneys and accountants.

HOW TO PROTECT YOURSELF

Read this part carefully. If you're going to jump into this business, you must treat it like a business. You must do some homework before each purchase.

Check the Property

You may buy a hundred mortgages and have nothing go wrong. But the potential exists that you might have to foreclose. If you have to foreclose, what do you own? Look at it this way: Anytime you buy a mortgage, assume you've bought the property. In other words, you must think enough of the property that you would buy it. You must like the neighborhood (since you're not going to move it), and you must like the condition of the property itself.

People are known by their habits. If the property is run-down and ill-kept, there is a good chance you will have trouble getting your payment on time. (The people don't assign much value to that, either.)

Determine Its Value

You probably won't have time for an appraisal. It's time consuming, it costs money, and if the mortgage is a great buy, it won't be around that long. Use the information in Chapter 20 to get a rough estimate of value in about 10 minutes, and you'll be fairly accurate. After you work a farm area for a while, you will know the values.

Look at the Numbers

There is some obvious risk to go with the large profits, but you can minimize it with a little knowledge. You need to know about loan-to-value ratios and discount-to-debt ratios.

The **loan-to-value (LTV) ratio** is a critical ratio. From time to time, real estate markets get soft (things just aren't selling). It seems to be happening about every five or six years. For a year or two, prices can actually drop. You do not want to be in a position where the drop in value wipes out all the owner's equity, leaving nothing to sit there and protect. You could end up with a lot of foreclosures. To avoid this, keep your LTV ratio at a maximum of 75 percent.

How do you determine it? Add all the loans up, and divide the total by the market value of the property. For example, in Figure 11E, a house has a value of $80,000, and the mortgages total $40,000 (a $30,000 first mortgage plus the $10,000 second you are buying). Divide $40,000 by $80,000 to get 0.5, or 50 percent. This is below the 75 percent figure, so it's OK.

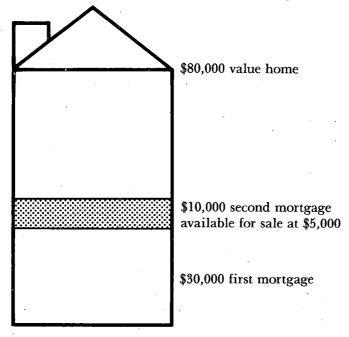

$80,000 value home

$10,000 second mortgage
available for sale at $5,000

$30,000 first mortgage

Figure 11E

The **discount-to-debt ratio** weighs the profit you are
making (the discount) against the total amount of debt in
the package. You get into high-risk areas when you take a
small profit (in terms of discount) against high existing
senior mortgages on the property. Therefore, keep this ratio
at about 15 percent. If you're conservative, use a 20 percent
figure.

In the illustration, if you were getting a $5,000 discount
on the $10,000 mortgage, and your remaining debt is
$30,000, to get your discount debt you would divide $5,000
(the discount) by $30,000 (the remaining debt). You get a
figure of 0.167, or 16.7 percent. It's above 15 percent, so it's
OK.

IT TAKES CASH

The bad news is, it takes cash; the good news is, it doesn't have to be your cash. There is a way to package the investment using another investor's cash, and there are ways you can raise cash by using your assets.

Use OPM

Use other people's money (OPM) to buy the mortgage. Though it's hard to believe, as people get wealthy, they tend to get a little lazy. They wouldn't mind making money, as long as they could find someone else to do the work. That someone could be you. For instance, if you could find an investor who would be happy with an 18 percent yield on his or her invested dollar, and you could find mortgages for sale at a 25 percent yield, there is a profit in that for you. The simple reason is that a 25 percent yield requires a higher discount than an 18 percent yield, and you can put the cash difference in your pocket.

Let's take an example: A $10,000 mortgage with a 15-year payout and a 10 percent interest rate would have to discount to $6,672 to yield 18 percent. To yield 25 percent, it would have to discount to $5,032. The difference, in your pocket, would be $1,640. Imagine what you could make working with the difference on a $50,000 or even a $100,000 mortgage. (Later on, this chapter tells you how to use a calculator to determine these amounts.)

Before you ever act as an agent to sell someone else's mortgage, check the laws in your state to find out what the requirements are to be a mortgage broker. A possible way around this is to always act as a principal (an owner). Write an offer to buy the mortgage at a discount (at, say, 25 percent) and sell it to your investor at a 20 percent discount. Remember to put "and/or assigns" in your contract after your name, and your escape clause could be "subject to partner's approval." You need to check this with a good attorney, but I don't know of any state in which a principal is prevented from selling his or her own asset.

By using a common escrow, the mortgage holder sells to you, and you sell to your investor in the same escrow. You would be able to pass any closing costs along to your investor. If you're cash-poor when you start, that can be a big help. The whole process is to become a good packager. When you have accomplished this, you can make money just by bringing your knowledge to a transaction.

Use Your Home

Don't go out and put a second mortgage on your home and use that money to buy discounted mortgages. It's too expensive. You must borrow all the money at once, you are paying interest on the whole sum, and you must pay it even if you haven't found a mortgage to buy yet.

Look at setting up a line of credit, using your home equity as collateral. If you have good credit and a decent job, you can go to many banks and S&Ls and set up a credit line. You normally have to pay a front fee of around 2 percent of the credit line, but you pay rent on the money only while you are using it. In other words, if a mortgage you bought pays off, you give the bank back the money, and you don't pay any rent until you find another mortgage to buy.

How much can you borrow? Usually up to 75 percent of the value of your home, less any existing mortgage. For example, if your home is worth $100,000 and your current first mortgage is $40,000, 75 percent of the value would be $75,000, and your line of credit would be $35,000 ($75,000 minus $40,000). There are upper limits, but they vary from institution to institution.

Merrill Lynch has a plan called Equity Access. They claim the credit lines could run up to $1 million, if the equity is there. There is more good news. Although you must make monthly interest payments, you don't have to pay off the principal for *ten* years with the Merrill Lynch account. Imagine buying mortgages, having them pay off, buying another, taking the money in and out as you need it, and you would only have to make sure after eight or nine years that enough mortgages were cashed out to pay off the principal. The clock would then start all over again, and you could take another decade. On the average, the interest rate is about 2 percent over prime.

Please, shop for the money. Different institutions have different rates. Pick up your Yellow Pages; call banks, S&Ls, and brokers; and ask them what they charge. Many of them will send you brochures on their program. Spend a few days looking at them and then pick the best. Besides your initial outlay, you don't pay anything until you start to use the money. We'll talk about another use for this cash in Chapter 15.

Unsecured Credit

Perhaps you have unsecured lines of credit. Here's some food for thought: What if you had a $10,000 line of credit? What if you went out into the marketplace and bought a $15,000 mortgage at discount for $10,000? You have now used up your personal line of credit.

You could bring in the mortgage and pledge it as collateral. The unsecured line of credit now becomes secured. Wouldn't that open up your unsecured line of credit again? You could go out and buy another $15,000 mortgage for $10,000 and take it to your bank, and so on.

A SERIOUS MONEY MAKER

Another concept works if you have access to a multiple-listing book. You would either have to be a member of the multiple-listing service (MLS) or have a friend with access to the book. You're interested in what houses are for sale. The book and courthouse records can identify private mortgages (potential discounts).

You want to inquire about buying these mortgages. Actually, you don't want to buy them, you want to get an option to buy. Let's say you would pay a $100 option fee (to be applied to the purchase price), for the right to buy a mortgage at a given percentage of value for the next six months. Let's say the mortgage is $10,000 and the discount agreed upon is $3,000. You record your option and wait. When the house sells, and a new loan is put on, the $10,000 mortgage is cashed out. You get $3,000, and the owner gets $7,000. What if you had 20 options going and 70 percent of the houses sold?

Two things are obvious here:

1. Do this only in times of low interest rates, which is when many homes are refinanced at time of sale.
2. Don't take an option on a second mortgage where there is an existing FHA or VA first mortgage sitting underneath it. These loans are too easy to assume, and chances are the mortgage you are optioning will not be cashed out.

This is really just one more way to make money.

WHAT'S A DISCOUNT?

If you are going to work in this lucrative field, you must learn to calculate discounts, yields, and payments. This may sound daunting, but there's some good news. In this great age of electronics, there is a wonderful machine that will do it for you. Go out and invest $30 or $40 in a business calculator. I use a Texas Instruments 11, but there are many models. Shop a few discount stores, and pick one out that you like. In about an hour, following the directions in the book that comes with the calculator, you can become pretty proficient.

The math involves only four basic numbers: the number of payments left (expressed as N on the calculator), the mortgage interest rate (expressed as %i), the monthly payment on the mortgage (*PMT*), and its present value (*PV*). If you know any three of the items, you can insert them into the calculator, punch a button, and the calculator will give you the fourth item.

Just think about it: If you had a $10,000 mortgage paying 10 percent interest, with 120 months left to pay (10 years), and you wanted a 20 percent yield on your money (percent return, or interest), all you would have to do is plug in the interest, number of payments, and the monthly payment; punch a button; and the calculator would display the price you could pay for the mortgage to get that return. If you wanted to see what price to pay for a 25 percent yield, you would just redo the problem with that interest rate. The difference between the two numbers could be your profit if you were working with an investor.

A MONEY-MAKING IDEA

Here's one of the easiest selling jobs in the world. It will let you raise the value of the mortgage, greatly increase your yield, and at the same time save people thousands of dollars. How's that for win/win? This may seem a little crazy, but, believe me, it works.

Take the following example: You have bought a $10,000 mortgage, paying 10 percent interest, with 180 months (15 years) left to pay. Since you wanted a 25 percent yield, you plugged the numbers into your calculator and paid $5,032 for the mortgage. The monthly payments were 180 monthly payments of $107.46 per month. You go to the payer of the mortgage and you say, "Mr. Payer, if you can afford it, I'm going to make you an offer you can't refuse. If you pay off this mortgage as you originally planned, you will pay a total of $19,342.80. If you will double your payment, the loan will pay off in about 52 months. [This is easy to do on your calculator.] Doubling the payment would make it $214.92 per month. You would only pay a total of $11,175.84, and you would realize a saving of $8,167. And, as they say in the television sales commercials, that's not all. I want you,

Mr. Payer, to have more savings. If you will do that, I'm willing to halve your interest rate. I will make it 5 percent instead of 10 percent."

The only problem you may have is that it sounds too good to be true. You may hear, "Why would you do that?" Your answer is, "If it's paid off faster, my return is increased. It's good for both of us; it's win/win." Work it out on your calculator and see for yourself. For a $5,032 purchase price, and payment of $107.46 for 180 months, your yield is 25 percent. At a purchase price of $5,032 and a payment of $214.92 per month, even at 5 percent interest, your yield becomes a whopping 43 percent. If they can't afford double, prorate it. If they can handle 50% more payment, make the interest rate 7½% (in the above example).

ANOTHER MIND GAME

Why don't you help out your friends, relatives, co-workers, and other people you know? Are you going to let them let their money sit in those banks and savings and loan associations and draw a little interest, or would you like to double their return? Get a better retirement plan started for everybody. Let's say they were getting 8 percent interest on their money at the bank (you may have to adjust this, based on prevailing interest rates at the time you read this book). You say, "Come with me, and I'll get you 16 percent interest, and I'll do all the work."

You sell half of the mortgage you just increased the value of in the previous example. Remember, after you increased the payment, your yield on the mortgage was a whopping 43 percent, and you paid $5,032. If you reduce the yield to 16 percent, half of the mortgage would sell, at discount, for $4,032. They would now get $107.46 per month, and you would get the same. What do you have left in your half of the mortgage? Well, you have $1,000 ($5,032 minus $4,032). With only that much money invested, your yield jumps to 125 percent.

Could you take these mortgages down to the bank and

borrow money against them? Of course—they're collateral. You could borrow money at 12 to 14 percent and lend it out at 40 percent or more. The possibilities are mind-boggling.

WHAT ABOUT PITFALLS?

There are two things to be wary of: First, at some time, regardless of how cautious you are, you may have to foreclose on a property. Even though it's a great property, and you will make money on the equity you gain, you still have to bear the expense of doing it. Not only are there expenses, but you must make up any payments and make additional payments during the foreclosure period. Don't sink every last penny into mortgages and have nothing in reserve. Keep about 10 percent of your cash in a reserve account to handle emergencies. It's just good business practice.

Second, beware the house-of-cards effect, where you borrow and lend, borrow and lend, and build up an empire that might come crashing down. The only thing that's going to kill you is greed. Stay within reasonable limits, and you can build a large estate over the next decade. It's trying to do it in one or two years that can give you problems.

THE MAIN POINT

If nothing else, I want you to remember this: *Never cash out a mortgage without asking for a discount.* It can cost you literally thousands of dollars. If you get only a $500 cash discount, that's certainly worth a phone call. You could get thousands off, and that's cash profit right in your pocket.

————————————————————

CHAPTER TWELVE

The Branches of the Tree

What is real estate ownership? I've asked that question countless times over the years, and I must have heard 50 different answers. Many of those answers were descriptions of what real estate *ownership* is. It is simply a bundle of rights, nothing more. Think of it as a tree with many branches, and each one of those branches is one of the rights.

When you look at it that way, you are presented with opportunities to get creative. It is quite possible to take just one of those branches and either pay for the whole tree, or use the branch for the down payment, which allows you to buy the property with none of your money. This alone can remove most of the excuses for not buying real estate. After all, who do you know who can't afford nothing down?

Take one example that's done all the time, and yet doesn't come to mind: the right of quiet possession. You give up that right when you rent the property. And yet you keep all the other rights. The tenant moves in and pays monthly rent. You take that rent and make a mortgage payment with it. You keep doing this until the mortgage payments run out and you own the building free and clear. Although it may take 20 or 25 years, haven't you purchased the entire property by just giving up one of your rights of ownership?

Although this chapter will give you some examples, don't limit yourself to them. They are merely there to stimulate your mind. From this day forward, don't just look at the tree, examine the branches. A little twig, properly used, can be worth a lot of money. ,

VALUABLE TREES

A cash-poor but creative investor was interested in buying a small investment property. She found she could not budge the owner; the owner had to have $2,000 in cash. That may not sound like much to buy a nice piece of property, but when you're cash-poor, it can look like Mt. Everest. While walking out of the property, a little dejected, the investor glanced at the two beautiful trees in the front yard. Looking a little closer, and then checking with a tree expert friend to be sure, she discovered they were black walnut trees.

Realizing this was very valuable wood, and they were very large trees, she contacted a cabinet maker. Bringing him to the site, she offered to sell the trees to him for $3,000 (not a bad asking price for trees you don't even own). The cabinet maker, being a smooth talker and a good negotiator, gradually, over the investor's many objections, got her down to $2,000.

The investor then had the ingredients for her deal. Is there a catch here? You have to sell the trees to get the down payment for the building, and you can't sell the trees before you own them. Impossible? Not at all. This is the stuff for which escrow companies were made. An escrow company is a neutral depository that holds all the elements of a transaction to make sure everybody gets what they are supposed to get. (If you live in a nonescrow state, this can be done at a standard real estate closing.) Figure 12A will give you a clear picture of how it works. Who loses? Nobody. The seller got what he wanted (cash plus mortgages for the balance of his equity), the buyer got what she wanted (the property without any of her cash down), and the cabinet maker got what he wanted (wood to build cabinets with). The whole transaction was win/win.

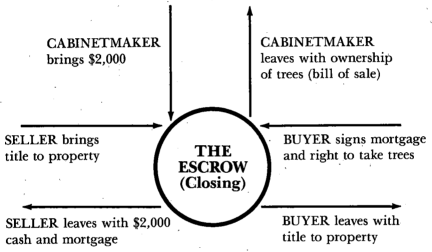

CABINETMAKER
brings $2,000

CABINETMAKER
leaves with ownership
of trees (bill of sale)

SELLER brings
title to property

THE
ESCROW
(Closing)

BUYER signs mortgage
and right to take trees

SELLER leaves with $2,000
cash and mortgage

BUYER leaves with
title to property

Figure 12A

SELLING THE FURNITURE AND HAVING IT TOO

Another investor was negotiating to buy a large furnished apartment building. Although the seller was flexible and willing to carry a lot of paper, the investor found he needed $20,000 in cash to put the transaction together. He stood back from the tree, and looked at the branches. "What about the furniture?" he thought. "I could sell the furniture and raise the cash I need to make the down payment." Then he thought, "If the tenants come home from work one

day and all the furniture is missing, I'm going to have some
very steamed tenants sitting around on the floor. What I
really need to do is sell the furniture and still keep it. Is this
possible? Of course—it's done all the time."

The investor contacted a leasing agent. He agreed to sell
the furniture to the agent for cash, and then lease it back
from the agent, with an option to buy (for a small payment)
after a few years.

Again, the investor used an escrow to satisfy all the
parties. Take a look at Figure 12B, and you will see how it
is put together.

LEASING AGENT
brings $20,000

LEASING AGENT leaves
with signed lease
from buyer

SELLER brings
title to property

**THE
ESCROW
(Closing)**

BUYER signs mortgage
and lease for furniture

SELLER leaves with
$20,000 and a mortgage

BUYER leaves with
title to property

Figure 12B

LEASE-OPTION TO SOLVE ALL PARTIES' PROBLEMS

Another cash-poor investor found a motivated seller
whose cash needs were $2,000 and couldn't be satisfied
otherwise. The seller had been unable to sell the house and
was willing to work with the investor in whatever way

possible. The investor, looking at the branches, asked permission to show the house to prospective tenants, and it was granted.

He then searched and found a couple who desperately wanted to be homeowners, and because of not having a lot of cash and being rejected by agents, were not hopeful of buying. The investor put together a lease with an option to buy the property for a higher price in a few years. The grateful couple were more than happy to pay a $2,000 option fee (to be applied to their purchase price down the road). Take a look at Figure 12C, and see how the escrow was put together.

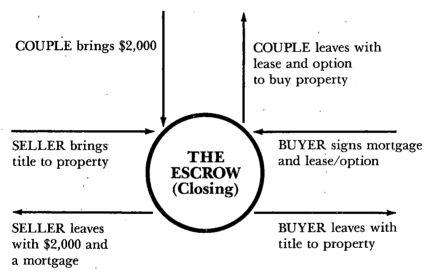

COUPLE brings $2,000

COUPLE leaves with
lease and option
to buy property

SELLER brings
title to property

THE ESCROW (Closing)

BUYER signs mortgage
and lease/option

SELLER leaves
with $2,000 and
a mortgage

BUYER leaves with
title to property

Figure 12C

BRINGING IN A HIGH-INCOME INVESTOR

Another investor had agreed to purchase a $100,000 piece of residential income property. The seller had been very flexible, and the financing package was great. He had bought the property for nothing down at a price $20,000 below market. It broke even in terms of cash flow, and it provided tax shelter. (Under the 1986 tax law changes and assuming a $20,000 value for land, the write-off would be $2,909.) There was only one problem: The investor had a very low income and had no need for tax shelter. His need was for extra income. He found someone in a higher tax bracket. (Someone with income of less than $100,000 per year is preferred, because of the phase-out provision of the maximum $25,000 allowable deduction.) The higher-income individual can use the tax shelter.

The investor sold the building to the person in the higher tax bracket and took back an option for five years to buy half of the building for no down payment at his original sales price. Since the building hadn't closed, he was able to get the high-income investor to complete the purchase and pay the closing costs. The sale to the higher-bracket individual was on the same terms as his purchase, with an additional payment of $10,500, payable at $3,500 per year for 3 years to the original investor. The individual in the high-income bracket gets a $2,909 tax deduction each year. Being in a 28-percent tax bracket, she would get tax savings of $814 per year. This individual also gets additional write-offs down the road after her yearly down payment ($3,500) stops, and she gets two bonuses:

1. Half of the appreciation at time of sale
2. A $10,000 bonus because the property was purchased $20,000 under market value

The original investor takes back his half of the building after five years, using his option. He gets cash flow in the beginning ($3,500 per year) and profit down the road. **Note:** The higher-bracket individual must comply with the hand-on management provision of the new tax code to get the depreciation offset of other income.

ANOTHER INVESTOR BUYS; YOU TAKE AN OPTION

Take a look at Figure 12D. You have located a $100,000 property for sale, from a motivated seller, who has to have a $15,000 down payment. She is willing to carry the remaining $85,000 in the form of a low-interest first mortgage. You find an investor with $15,000 cash who will buy

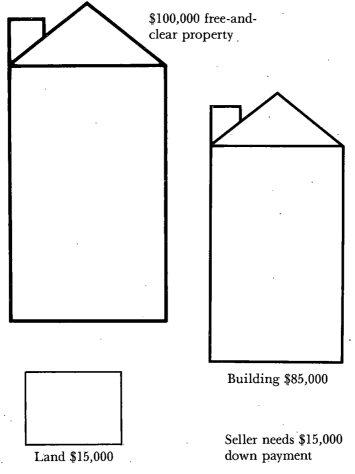

$100,000 free-and-clear property

Building $85,000

Land $15,000

Seller needs $15,000 down payment

Figure 12D

the land and lease it back to you at a fair return (say, 10 percent, or whatever is reasonable now). You would also get an option to buy the land back, at appraised value, after a few years. This could be done by refinancing the total property (land plus building). Figure 12E shows the escrow.

Figure 12E

CONCLUSION

There are many ways to put a transaction together and many ways to generate cash using the investment itself. Anytime you find an investment that comes with a separate piece of land, you have found a prime candidate. See if the separate piece can't be sold (as part of the closing), and use the proceeds to either buy the remaining part or to at least provide the down payment. Before you walk away from a motivated seller, see if you can't satisfy his or her needs by breaking off a branch.

CHAPTER THIRTEEN

Miscellaneous Money Makers

This chapter is a collection of tools you can use to make additional profits in real estate. You needn't use them all at once, but be familiar with them. As you work in the marketplace, you can incorporate them as the situations present themselves.

THE WRAPAROUND MORTGAGE

The wraparound mortgage is a greatly misunderstood money-making vehicle. Many people confuse it with a blanket mortgage (a mortgage or trust deed that sits on more than one piece of property). A wraparound mortgage is a subordinate mortgage that sits on top of one of more senior mortgages. It has two major benefits to you as a seller:

1. *Safety*—You will always know the other mortgages have been paid on the property, since you will be paying them.

2. *Yield*—You can increase the yield on your equity to over 20 percent though the interest rate on your mortgage is much lower.

A wraparound is always easier to explain with a diagram than it is verbally. Look at Figure 13A. You have a $100,000 property to sell. It has an existing $50,000 FHA first mortgage and a $20,000 second mortgage carried back by the person who sold the property to you. You have $30,000 in equity.

Now look at two different ways to sell it, and you'll see the advantage of the wraparound mortgage. In case A, you sell with a $10,000 cash down payment, the buyer assumes the first and second mortgages, and you carry back a third mortgage of $20,000. The interest rate on the older FHA loan is 9 percent, the seller carried back the second for 10 percent, and you get 12 percent interest on your third mortgage. In case B, you take the same $10,000 down payment and put a $90,000 all-inclusive mortgage or deed of trust on the property. The interest rate is still 12 percent.

Look at the difference in return. In case A, your yield is 12 percent, which is the interest rate on your third mortgage. In case B, you have some bonuses. You are also collecting 12 percent interest on the $50,000 that represents the first mortgage, but you are paying only 9 percent interest. You make an extra 3 percent interest. Three percent of $50,000 is $1,500 per year extra interest. On the $20,000 representing the second mortgage, you are paying 10 percent interest, and you are collecting 12 percent interest also. That's a bonus of $400 (2 percent of $20,000).

Let's see what the true yield is on your $20,000 equity:

$2,400	Interest of 12% on your $20,000 equity
1,500	Extra interest of 3% on $50,000 first mortgage
400	Extra interest of 2% on $20,000 second mortgage
$4,300	TOTAL

The return on your equity is:

$$\frac{\text{return}}{\text{equity}} = \frac{\$4,300}{\$20,000} = 21.5\% \text{ return on equity}$$

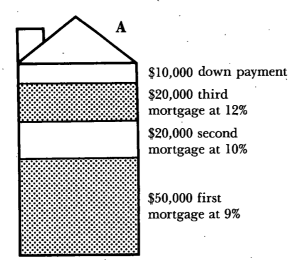

A

$10,000 down payment

$20,000 third
mortgage at 12%

$20,000 second
mortgage at 10%

$50,000 first
mortgage at 9%

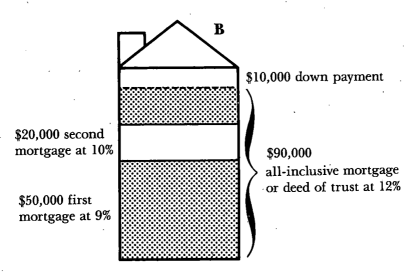

B

$10,000 down payment

$20,000 second
mortgage at 10%

$50,000 first
mortgage at 9%

$90,000
all-inclusive mortgage
or deed of trust at 12%

Figure 13A

To make this work, the underlying mortgages must be free of due-on-sale clauses. When you have FHA or VA mortgages, and any seconds are owner carrybacks without due-on-sale clauses, you have the ingredients to make it work. Note that using a wraparound at a higher interest rate enables you to buy houses and sell them for the same price you paid for them, and retire on the extra income. Three percent extra interest on $1 million worth of mortgages (on houses you bought and sold) would be $30,000 extra income per year. This could come in for 10 or 15 years or more (the length of the mortgage).

SUBSTITUTION OF COLLATERAL

Substitution of collateral is a clause, put into the original purchase agreement, that lets you change collateral for the mortgage the seller is carrying back. It might read something like: "The buyer shall have the right to substitute collateral of equal or greater value for this mortgage." The seller may insist on having the right to approve the other property. In that case you add, "not to be unreasonably withheld." Check with your attorney on the wording.

Let's look at the down-the-road benefit. You buy a $90,000 property for $10,000 down, assume a $50,000 first mortgage, and the seller carries back a $30,000 second mortgage. Down the road a few years (whatever it takes), your property is now worth $130,000 (see Figure 13B) and you want to raise some cash. The rents are now up and can carry a higher payment, so you decide to refinance the property. You find you can get a new 80 percent loan of $104,000. The $30,000 second mortgage has been paid down to $25,000, and the first has been paid down to $40,000.

The normal procedure would be to pay off the first and second for $65,000 ($40,000 plus $25,000) and put the balance of $39,000 ($104,000 new loan, minus $65,000 payoff) in your pocket. Instead, using the substitution-of-collateral clause, you transfer the second mortgage to a

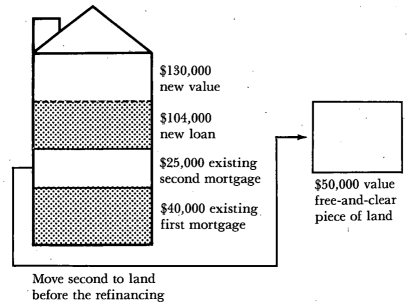

$130,000
new value

$104,000
new loan

$25,000 existing
second mortgage

$40,000 existing
first mortgage

$50,000 value
free-and-clear
piece of land

Move second to land
before the refinancing

Figure 13B

$50,000 free-and-clear piece of land you own. This gives
you three benefits:

1. You save a low-interest $25,000 older loan.
2. You put an extra $25,000 cash into your pocket
   because you didn't have to cash out the second
   mortgage.
3. You get a low-interest-rate loan on a piece of raw land.

How do you convince the seller to take the clause if he or
she objects to it? You sell it as a benefit and not as a liability.
You might say to the seller, "This mortgage is my obligation, and I want to make sure it gets paid. You trust me,
since you're giving me this mortgage, and I want to make
sure the payments are always on time. If I sell this property
down the road, I'm going to place this mortgage on another
one of my properties, so I can make sure you always get
your payments."

MORTGAGE WALKING

You walk your dog; why not walk your mortgage? This is done at the time of purchase, rather than at a later date. Moving or walking a mortgage can overcome a lender's objection to funding a load (instead of no down payment, your down payment is equity in other property), and it can put cash in your pocket at the same time.

Take a look at Figure 13C. You are going to buy property B from a seller. You are going to arrange for a new $60,000 mortgage on property B. The seller agrees, as a part of her $100,000 compensation, to carry a mortgage for $60,000. To avoid overfinancing, you move the $60,000 mortgage the seller is carrying to your $150,000 property A with an existing $60,000 first mortgage. The seller will get, as her balance, $40,000 in cash.

Look at Figure 13D to see where you end up. The seller gets $40,000 in cash, plus a $60,000 second mortgage on property A (a total of $100,000, the price of her property). You get $20,000 in cash ($60,000 new loan, less $40,000 cash to seller) and a $40,000 built-in equity in property B. What did you accomplish? You took cash out of a closing as a buyer, without overfinancing the property.

THE SUBORDINATION CLAUSE

The subordination clause lets the seller's mortgage remain with the property, but it lets you take cash out of the property through a refinance without cashing out the seller's mortgage. It might read something like: "The seller's loan shall be subordinate to the existing first mortgage or any renewal, extension, or replacement thereof." Check with your attorney.

For an example, look at Figure 13E. You buy a property from a motivated seller for $100,000. You assume an existing FHA first mortgage, and the seller carries back a $40,000 second mortgage for his equity. About 10 years go by, and

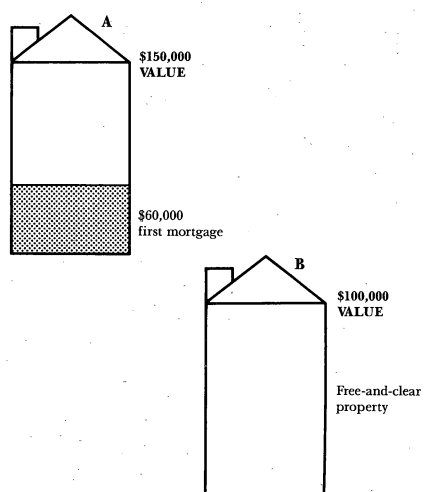

$150,000
VALUE

$60,000
first mortgage

$100,000
VALUE

Free-and-clear
property

Before Transaction

Figure 13C

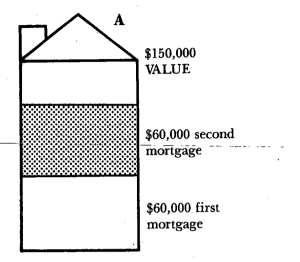

$150,000
VALUE

$60,000 second
mortgage

$60,000 first
mortgage

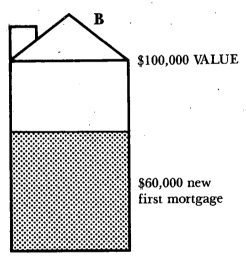

$100,000 VALUE

$60,000 new
first mortgage

After Transaction

Figure 13D

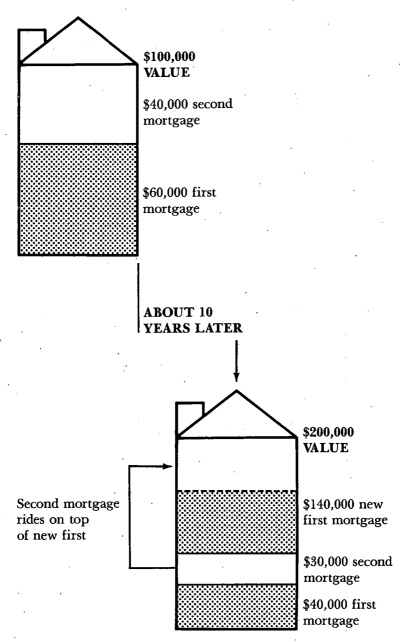

Figure 13E

the property is now worth $200,000. It's time to reap the harvest a little. You go out and get a new $140,000 loan on the property. The seller's loan (paid down to $30,000), instead of having to be cashed out, rides up on top of the new $140,000 mortgage, giving you an extra $30,000 in cash. Remember, borrowed dollars are tax-free dollars, which makes them even better. No tax is due until you sell.

CASH CRANKERS

Here are some creative ideas on ways to use cash to amplify the amount of equity you create when you buy property:

- Buy mortgages at deep discount and offer the mortgage at full face value for a down payment.
- Buy real estate at deep discount from motivated sellers and sell at retail on very soft terms (you carry paper). When possible, use a wraparound mortgage to increase your profits.
- Buy bonds at deep discount and offer them at retail as a down payment on real estate.
- Buy cars, boats, travel trailers, etc., at tax sales at deep discount and offer them, at retail, as a down payment on real estate.

USE A MORATORIUM

A moratorium can work when a seller overprices a property. Say a property is worth $70,000; however, the seller wants $75,000 and won't budge. Say to the seller, "I'll pay your price, if you will give me a moratorium on payments for 2 years." (This means no payments on the mortgage.) Ask for 2 years; you might settle for 6, 12, or 18 months.

The benefit is that you rent for $600 a month (if that's the market rent) and collect $600 times 24 months, or $14,400 in cash as a trade-off for paying too much for the property.

CASH FROM A MORTGAGE

Here are five ways to get cash from a mortgage you own:

1. Sell the note. If you have an $80,000 note, you might sell it for, say, $50,000. This is the least desirable way to raise cash, since you take the biggest loss.
2. Sell the payments. If the mortgage is bringing in $800 per month for the next 36 months (a total of $28,000), you might sell those payments for, say, $20,000. This is better than 1, because you lose only $8,000 instead of $30,000.
3. Sell part interest. Sell one-half of the note for, say, $25,000 to raise cash. This cuts your discount in half to $15,000 instead of $30,000.

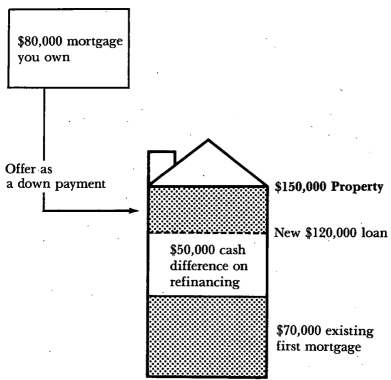

Figure 13F

4. Pledge it as collateral at the bank. Take the $80,000 mortgage to the bank and borrow $50,000 on it. This way you don't have to take a discount.
5. Use it as a down payment and then refinance the property. This is illustrated in the figure 13F. You offer an $80,000 mortgage you own on a property with an $80,000 equity ($150,000 value minus the $70,000 existing loan). You then refinance the property for $120,000 and put $50,000 in your pocket ($120,000 minus the $70,000 existing loan). You get about as much cash as you could have sold the mortgage for, and you still own a building with $30,000 equity ($150,000 minus the new loan of $120,000).

Learning to Use Your Dead Equities

Dead equity comes from two different sources. One is the portion of the property the lender won't lend on. If you had a $100,000 rental house and you went out to get a loan, you'd find out you can't get a $100,000 loan. The loan officer will give you an $80,000 loan. This leaves $20,000 in "unlendable" equity—hence the name dead equity.

The other source is dead, dead equity. For instance, it could be that piece of land you bought that is:

- 50 miles east of the boondocks
- A great investment at low tide
- Flood-free when it isn't raining
- Going to be great, if they ever locate water

You get the picture.

With a little creativity, you can use the unusable. You can also use the unsalable as a vehicle to make money. Let's look first at a way to use the "unlendable" portion of your investment real estate, and then at a creative way to get a low-interest loan on your land.

EQUITY TRANSFER

Figure 14A shows a $100,000 property with an $80,000 loan on it. You can't borrow anything through conventional lending sources. The question is, what can you do with the $20,000 of equity?

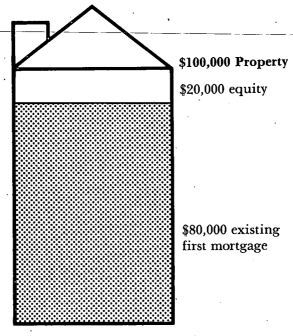

$100,000 Property

$20,000 equity

$80,000 existing first mortgage

Figure 14A

Find another $100,000 property with an $80,000 loan on it. Create a note, mortgage your property *A* (see Figure 14B), and offer that mortgage as a down payment on property *B*. Notice that this is a private mortgage on a property, not the "hard money" commercial variety. Is there anything that says the interest rate and the payment have to be at "market"? No. In fact, the more motivated the seller of property *B*, the better the terms you can get. Offer a low interest rate and a very low payment. You can always

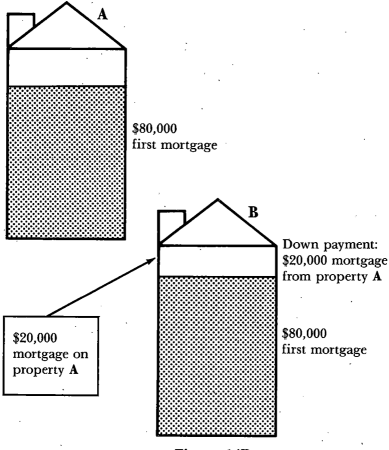

**$80,000
first mortgage**

**Down payment:
$20,000 mortgage
from property A**

**$20,000
mortgage on
property A**

**$80,000
first mortgage**

Figure 14B

negotiate up. Once you've made an offer and they accept it, you can't negotiate down.

The nice part is that you don't have to stop here. Any down payment, whether it's cash or paper, creates instant equity. If you make a $20,000 down payment on property *B*, you have $20,000 equity in property *B*. Why not create a note and mortgage on property *B* and offer that for a down payment on property *C*? And don't stop there. *A* buys *B*, *B* buys *C*, *C* buys *D*, *D* buys *E*, and so on (see Figure 14C). You

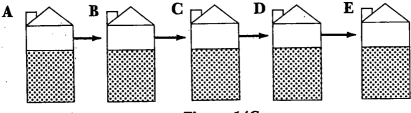

Figure 14C

could buy 10 or 20 properties or more using this simple equity-transfer technique. Have you ever been to a real estate lecture and they told you, "We'll teach you how to take the equity out of your property for about $10 and invest it in real estate"? Well, you just learned the big secret. The $10 is the recording fee it takes to record the mortgage you are giving for the down payment.

The problem you're going to encounter when you're creating 100 percent financing is negative cash flow. Unless you can get the seller to give at least a partial moratorium on payments, you will find the property has to be fed. For help with this problem, use the discussion on eliminating negative cash flow in Chapter 23. One solution would be to get an investor in a high tax bracket and give him or her half the property in return for carrying the negative cash flow until you can raise rents enough to eliminate it. Any equity you might have could be returned at sale, before you split any profit from appreciation.

USING YOUR LAND

You can use your land for equity transfer. Create your own note and mortgage, and offer it for a down payment on some other piece of property.

When you find a special circumstance, you can use it differently. Say you have a $60,000 piece of land that is free and clear of mortgages (not a requirement, but this arrangement works better if it is). You either bought it years ago and paid it off, or you bought it at a tax sale at pennies on the dollar. You find a seller who is unreasonable on price. She has a $100,000 piece of property for sale and will take $10,000 down; you can assume the $60,000 FHA first mortgage, and the seller is willing to carry back a $30,000 second mortgage at a low interest rate.

You know, and she normally does also, that the property is either overpriced or, at the least, at the very top of the market. She is set, and you just can't budge her. Here we try the routine that goes, "If you'll do something for me, I'll do something for you." You say, "Ms. Seller, I'll agree to your price and terms on one condition. If you'll let me put the

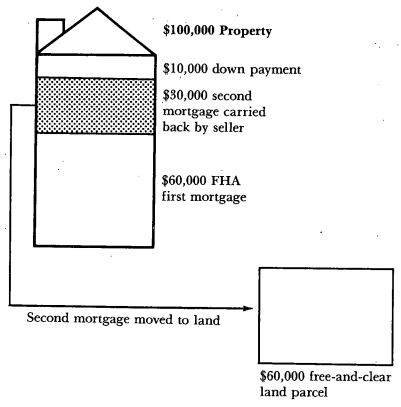

$100,000 Property

$10,000 down payment

$30,000 second
mortgage carried
back by seller

$60,000 FHA
first mortgage

Second mortgage moved to land

$60,000 free-and-clear
land parcel

Figure 14D

second mortgage you're carrying back on my $60,000 piece of land instead of on your property."

Figure 14D shows some obvious benefits to point out to the seller. She still gets her $10,000 cash, but instead of having only $10,000 in equity standing behind her second mortgage, she now has $30,000 in land equity. Instead of having a second-mortgage position, she now has a first-mortgage position. And she gets the price she wants for the property—a price she may be having second thoughts about ever getting.

You get a low-interest loan on your piece of land. You also get an additional $30,000 equity in a home. Down the road, the home can be refinanced. Unless it is in a prime location and you're willing to pay very high interest rates, the land is hopeless.

Never underestimate the benefit of assuming that a real estate problem can be solved and looking for a solution, instead of walking away with an attitude of "It can't be done." The difference in profit is enormous.

CHAPTER FIFTEEN

Fortunes in Foreclosures

One could write an entire book on the fortunes to be made in foreclosures and still fail to cover it completely. As a matter of fact, many people have. This chapter simply attempts to give you an understanding of the process and enough information to allow you to locate distressed properties and make some money on them. If you live in a major city, you will find there are thousands of them each year. By acquiring some basic knowledge, you will open a world of enormous profits.

THE FORECLOSURE PROCESS

Let's take a look at the basic process and understand what happens.

First, the buyer falls behind on his or her payments. The reasons are many: loss of job, living beyond one's means, or some other crisis. Initially, the homeowner may fall behind only one or two payments. But if you're finding it hard to make one house payment, imagine having to make two or three. The homeowner has the same problem. It is at this point that solving the problem is cheapest. It is just a matter of making up the back payments. If you can catch homeowners at this stage, you can pick up some great buys. On one of the first few houses I bought, I picked up $12,000 in equity simply by making up two back payments. The people just wanted out from under their problem.

Then the lender sends letters. If you have ever fallen behind on house payments, you will have noticed that mail starts to arrive. The first letter is always pleasant. "We haven't received your payment. If you have already sent it, please disregard this notice." The later letters start to get sharp; the wording is curt and to the point. "Action will have to be taken." This makes the homeowner worried and anxious about the need to eliminate the problem. Motivation increases. It is still a matter of clearing up some back payments and is a great time to approach the homeowner.

Then the lender sends out the final letter. It says to pay in 10 days or the matter will be turned over to an attorney. The fear of litigation enters the picture, and few homeowners are aware of the process or what comes next. This is still a good time to get involved, since both the homeowner and lender become motivated. Lenders rarely like to foreclose on properties, and they would welcome a white knight riding up to solve the problem.

Now an attorney enters the picture. Expenses start to mount. To correct the situation, you'll need back payments plus attorney's and other fees—maybe $1,500 to $2,000. If you have cash and there is $10,000 or more equity in the property, this is good use of your time.

Next, public notice is filed. The world is alerted to the problem; it all becomes public record. Professional investors who work the foreclosure market get involved. Several people may contact the homeowner, wanting to solve his or her problem.

Finally, there's a public sale on the courthouse steps. The

house is auctioned off. Only the mortgage being foreclosed on and any senior liens are saved. In other words, a person with a second mortgage must cure the first mortgage (make up back payments) and foreclose him- or herself. The mortgage holder can bid up to the amount of the mortgage without putting up any cash, which is not the case for other bidders. If you are planning to work these sales, you should go to at least two without bidding, just to see what is going on. You may notice the same people at these sales bidding over and over. Some of them may be working together. Keep your eyes open.

WHERE TO FIND FORECLOSURES

There are many ways to find foreclosures. This section briefly introduces the major ways.

Legal Notices

There are legal papers in your areas that publish foreclosure notices. Your attorney, your banker, or your real estate broker can usually tell you the names of local papers and how to subscribe to them. In some cases, these notices may be published in your local paper.

Attorneys

Some attorneys specialize in handling foreclosures. When you contact them, don't expect a glad hand. You may be able to get most of the information you need from their secretaries, leaving only one or two questions for them.

Realtors

Local real estate brokers normally have access to available foreclosures. They also have listings or knowledge of people who are in trouble. One of the things an owner does when behind in his or her payments is to call a broker and see if the broker can sell it. There is rarely enough time. If you stress to the broker that you can move quickly and work out a way for the broker to get compensated for his or her effort, it is quite possible to work with him or her.

Active Searching

The simple process of expanding yourself will put you in contact with problem situations. I got a great buy on a behind-in-the-payments situation from a broker from whom I had purchased another house. I had told him that if he had a situation that required fast action, I was his man. All he had to do was call me. We closed in five days, which was not bad. The existing loan was an FHA loan, so I only had to make up the two payments behind and take it over. Needless to say, when the broker found another situation, he called me again.

Advertising Yourself

Don't keep it a secret that you buy real estate. Circulating flyers or just the process of running simple classified ads in the paper can bring you some business. Ads like: "Behind in your payments? Save your credit. Call ———." Even "I buy homes" can bring telephone calls from sellers who are in trouble.

Business Cards

Get 500 business cards printed and circulate them. When you have passed out a lot of cards, your phone will start to ring. At parties, when people ask what you do, hand them a business card saying you buy real estate. This will make you a lot more money than telling them you make widgets (or whatever your other occupation is).

THE SIX STEPS

Let's take a look at the process of buying a foreclosure once it has entered default. You have been alerted by the notice of default filed at the courthouse, and you go through a specific process to determine whether you want to buy the property.

Step 1: Inspect

The first thing you do is go out and look at the property, the general condition of the outside. Eventually, you will be able to estimate what it will take to correct any problems. Next, you look at the thing you can't correct, the neighborhood. It should be middle-class at least, and a place you should be reasonably comfortable in after dark. Your potential buyer or renter will certainly want to be. If it needs a complete paint job and major yard work and you're cash poor, you might decide to pass (unless you have a financial partner). Always pass on the bad neighborhood; you can't correct it.

Step 2: Attorney

Contact the attorney in charge. You want to find out as much as you can about the house and the financing (what the existing mortgages are and their monthly payments). Then you want to find out the "cure" amount—how much actual cash it will take to bring the property out of foreclosure.

Step 3: The Prelim

Get a preliminary title report; this is crucial. It will tell you the amount of the loans and whether there are any other liens against the property (IRS, property tax, mechanics', or other liens). If the house is a financial mess, it is almost always better to pass and go on to deals that are less complicated. You could spend months on a mess and get nothing. Life's too short for that.

Step 4: The Owner

The next step is to talk directly to the owner and work out whatever agreement you can. If the house is vacant, see the discussion later in this chapter on how to find the owner. (These will be many of your best buys, because the owner is less likely to have been talked to by others if the house is vacant.) You can explain what is going to happen to the owner and his or her credit if he or she doesn't handle this situation.

Step 5: Quitclaim Deed

Have the owner sign a quitclaim deed in return for whatever compensation you have agreed upon. When recorded, this will give you his or her interest in the property.

Step 6: Notification

Notify the bank and attorney. Let them know that the matter has been resolved and the loans will be brought current.

THE CONVENTIONAL LENDER

If the existing first mortgage is an FHA or VA loan, it is a fairly simple matter to make up the back payments and take over the loan. If the loan is with a bank or savings and loan association, it is a good idea to speak with the lender about taking over the loan and making it current. Most lenders want to avoid foreclosing and are glad to have the problem solved.

You will meet exceptions to the rule. If you encounter hostility when you're trying to take over a loan of someone behind in his or her payments, you might say, "If we can't work this out, the owner may well have to file bankruptcy." In most cases, this will soften up the lender.

Don't let lenders stick you with a lot of fees or a higher interest rate. Just remember who's doing whom the favor.

A SIMPLE LETTER

One way to work the notices of default on homes is simply to send a letter to the various homeowners. An example of such a letter is shown in the accompanying illustration.

John and Mary Smith
312 Main Street
Anywhere, USA

Dear Mr. and Mrs. Smith,

You have been, or soon will be, notified that your home is in foreclosure. This can be embarrassing and can also seriously damage your credit. But your situation is far from hopeless. There is no need to lose your home by having the sheriff put you out in the street.

Retain your ability to buy another home in the future. I can arrange it so you can continue to live in the property, and no one will know you no longer own it. I have helped others, and I can help you. Call me as soon as possible at 888-9999.

Regards,

Edward Investor

Sometimes people in default become able to make payments, but not to make up the back payments. This makes them good prospects to rent the property back from you after you buy it. No one has to know that title has changed hands, and they can continue to live there.

GET FORECLOSED PROPERTY WITH A MORTGAGE

Some properties have a first mortgage, a small second, and a large amount of equity. You may find the holder of a small second who is dreading the thought of having to foreclose. Running a simple ad in the paper could bear fruit:

> I buy bad paper.
> Hollis, 888-9999

You might buy the small second at a good discount. (Why not—it's bad, isn't it?) Then you would have at least two options:

1. Talk directly to the homeowner from a position of strength. You are the mortgage holder, the person with the power to foreclose. You might take over the house by paying the owner a small amount for his or her equity.
2. Reinstate the first mortgage and foreclose yourself. At the auction, bid the amount of your mortgage with no additional cash out of your pocket. If there are no other bidders, you would have the house. If there are, you would get the full amount of your second mortgage, which you bought at discount.

AFTER THE FACT

There is profit still to be made after the lender has taken back the property. Lenders do not want to be property owners. Owning property reduces the monies they can get from the Federal Reserve Board, and in severe cases can threaten their charter. They are not equipped to manage property and would like to get rid of it.

Lenders call these properties REOs (real estate owned). A specific officer in the bank handles REOs. But don't call him and say, "Do you have any REOs?" He or she gets five or six of those calls every week and will say, "No, we don't have any right now."

Represent yourself as a problem solver. You can handle any difficult problems the officer might have. Use what you have learned in this book to solve this person's problems. You are then in a position to get some of the "cream" of his or her portfolio. The key is to get in the door and establish the relationship. Meet face to face and discuss his or her problems.

THE GOVERNMENT

Thousands of foreclosures are sitting in the various government agencies. FHA foreclosures alone are enormous. Contact your local office of the Department of Housing and Urban Development (HUD) about information and being placed on a mailing list for new foreclosures.

The Veterans Administration has a large inventory of foreclosures, although they don't treat investors very kindly. If you are looking for a home of your own, however, they can be a very good source. Because VA loans may be for 100 percent of the property's value, a veteran may have little equity in the house. Such a person is not very motivated to stick with it through hard times.

REDEMPTION RIGHTS

If you're going to buy foreclosures, you should be aware of redemption rights. An owner usually has up to one year after a judicial foreclosure (through the courts) to recover the property by paying what is owed, plus interest, costs, and penalties. He or she can remain in possession by paying reasonable rent during this period.

Under a trust deed, there are usually no redemption rights after a trustee's sale. Nor are there usually redemption rights under a land contract. It would pay you to check on your state law before you start to buy, bid, or make offers.

OCCUPIED VS. VACANT

Houses will be either occupied or vacant. When you are dealing with an occupied house, you are dealing with a person's home and all the emotion that goes with owning it. You must first convince the people that something bad is happening to them. You may show that person the published notice of default and still be unable to convince them they are going to lose it. They are sure some miracle is going to happen and the home will be saved. They may look at you as a vulture coming to pick the bones of the dead. You're going to meet hostility, distrust, fear, and competitors ("This other guy said he would . . ."). The profit is there; you just have to handle the problems that go along with it.

Vacant houses have several advantages. First, it's nobody's home. They are living somewhere else, and you don't have to encounter the emotions that accompany losing one's home. Second, if the owner isn't readily available and you must do some detective work, it's more likely that no one else has talked with him or her.

The best way to find empties is to drive neighborhoods and look for signs of neglect. Tall grass, broken windows, peeling paint, trash in the yard, or uncollected papers and mail. There may even be a For Sale or For Rent sign in the window, although often there is not.

Let's say you've found one; how do you find the owner? Here are some things to do:

1. Walk around and talk to the local kids. They will know who lived there, when they moved, where, and perhaps why. ("Their father lost his job.")
2. For more specific knowledge, knock on adjacent doors. To put the neighbor on your side, say, "The child I talked to said the Johnsons had moved to [name of place]. I'd like to buy their house and clean it up. It's a real eyesore." The neighbor may break an Olympic sprint record getting you the address and phone number. She doesn't like living next door to it, either. If she doesn't have the address or phone number, you might ask, "Do any of their relatives still live in the city?" You might pick up a brother or a cousin who would know how to contact them.
3. Go to the nearest post office, pay a $1 fee, and you can get their forwarding address. By filling out a simple form, you will have an address to write them a letter.
4. Go to the courthouse. Check to see if the address on the tax rolls has been changed. They won't get their tax bill if the county doesn't know where to send it.
5. If the address hasn't been changed, get the name of the lender from the courthouse. It is quite possible the lender has their address, since they will probably be sending in payments. Approach the lender with the fact the house is now vacant (he or she probably didn't know). Stress that you want to do something before problems develop (music to his or her ears). Ask the lender for the address in order to write about buying the house.
6. Attach to the front door a note with "Owner" printed on the outside. Express an interest in buying the house, and leave your phone number. It's possible the owners live within several miles and come every week or so to collect mail and check the place. You could get a phone call weeks later.
7. As a last resort, call all the people in the phone book with the same last name and see if they knew the

owners or are related. If your luck's good, the last name is unusual. If your luck is bad, the last name is Smith or Jones.

You might think of hiring "lookers" to do the locating work for you. These could be people you pay by the hour, or a flat fee for every house you buy that they find. A perfect person for this job is a mail carrier. Who would know better when a house went vacant? This advance knowledge could give you a head start on any competitors.

Finding foreclosures is a time-consuming process, and you will spend a lot of hours going up dead ends. However, you can quickly make a profit of $10,000 to $20,000 when you locate the right house. It's worth it. Good hunting.

———————————

CHAPTER SIXTEEN

Wealth-Building Fixer-Uppers

Building wealth through fixer-uppers is a major subject that could probably fill a book all by itself. Nevertheless, this chapter will give you a basic understanding of the subject. While you're looking at properties, you are going to come across houses and apartment buildings that need various repairs. You are going to be faced with deciding whether or not to buy.

SOME VARIABLES

Understanding some variables should help you make an intelligent decision. This chapter starts by describing elements associated with the house that are above and beyond the actual piece of real estate.

147

Neighborhood

The neighborhood is something you can't change. You could spend thousands of dollars fixing up a property and, if when you're finished it's still sitting among a lot of houses that look bad, you've probably wasted your money. An old adage in the fixer-upper business is still sound: Buy the worst house in the best neighborhood, not the other way around. A good evaluation for a neighborhood is whether you would be comfortable there after dark. If you would, it's probably OK. Stick with middle-class to upper-middle-class neighborhoods.

Financing

It makes no sense to dive in and spend money, time, and effort if you're walking into a nightmare. If the existing financing is all full of due-on-sale clauses and you have inflexible lenders, why bother? An exception might be if the homeowner was behind on the payments. This alone can motivate a lender to become reasonable. It's worth a call to one of the loan officers to see whether they will let you assume at the current rate (if it's reasonable) if you bring the loan current.

Area Rentals

You need to know what the house would rent for after it's fixed up. Will market rent carry the property, or will you have a negative cash flow? If you have negative cash flow, your package should include a plan to solve that. Play renter and shop the neighborhood rents.

Personal Property

What actually goes with the property? Be sure that it's written out in the purchase agreement. If things that you thought were going to be left are missing after the closing and you have nothing in writing, you're out of luck.

WHAT WILL IT COST?

You will need a reliable handyman who is capable of doing some minor repairs. Perhaps you'll even need more than one—this is an age of specialists. You can use contractors, but they are expensive. You may find yourself paying $20 to $30 an hour for labor costs, and that can eat up all your profit in a hurry.

Questioning real estate brokers and other investors should give you a good handyman. If you decide to do a number of fix-up projects, you could develop a full-time person. If you're a rookie and don't know housing, I would suggest you use a house inspector to evaluate your first few endeavors. You don't need any surprises.

THE FOUR-TO-ONE FORMULA

I have a strict formula with fixer-uppers. For every dollar I spend in fixing up the property, I want to make $4 in profit (cash or equity). There are people I know who work on a three-to-one and even two-to-one basis. My requirements are high because I don't care for fixer-uppers that much. I'm notorious for saying, "Hammers don't fit my hand; golf clubs fit."

The profit base of four to one must remain after all selling costs. The first fixer-upper I bought (about 12 years ago) required a little over $2,000, and the equity increase was $12,000. That's about six to one and well worth the effort. The ratio you work with is up to you and how well you take to fixer-uppers.

WHO BUYS HOUSES?

Wives buy homes; husbands come along for the ride. If you try to make it otherwise, you're going to be standing out in the cold whistling "Dixie." The two most important rooms are the kitchen and the bathroom. When you're dressing up the house, spend the most attention on these rooms. You can get a great return on your dollar.

DOLLAR-MAKING DEFECTS

Some defects are almost guaranteed to return more for fixing them than what it cost you. Following are some examples.

Paint

Nothing makes a house harder to sell than an obvious need for paint (outside and in). The mere dressing up of a coat of paint can drive the selling price of a house up thousands of dollars. Don't buy the most expensive paint you can find; you will only be paying for the advertising dollars of that company. Get a paint that is good enough to cover in one coat.

Use off-white paint for the inside; it goes with everything. Studies have shown that a house painted yellow outside sells better than any other color. Combine that with white trim, and you'll have a fast mover. Use enamel for the kitchen and bathrooms (moisture problems), and use latex on the rest. You will find that water-based paint cleans better than oil-based paint.

Landscape

Your property doesn't have to be in *Better Homes & Gardens,* but it does have to look nice if you're going to sell or rent it. If you're buying abandoned houses, one of the problems is grass that's a foot or two high. You must have the lawn mowed and the shrubs trimmed and weeded.

Hint: If you are trying to sell quickly, mow the lawn before closing. (It's a small expense.) The grass could take a couple of weeks to turn green.

Draperies

Dirty, torn, or sagging drapes seriously detract from a house for rent or for sale. You'd be amazed at how cheaply you can buy drapes. Stores like Penney's have outlet stores. Look in the Yellow Pages or call the main store and ask them where their outlet store is located. You can buy drapes and many other things at pennies on the dollar.

Carpet

Carpet that is worn out or uncleanable must be replaced. But give carpet a chance; it can fool you. The house I mentioned earlier had about an inch of dirt on the carpet. It was hard to tell there was a carpet. I took a spoon and scraped down and found a pretty decent carpet. It took my handyman three hours with a rented steam cleaner to get it all up, but it wasn't a major expense. I got quite a few more years out of the carpet. When you are buying, look for sales, discounts, and private carpet sellers with low overhead.

Light Fixtures

Houses are sold on a visual basis, and a few dollars spent on fancier fixtures can motivate a buyer. Again, shop the outlet stores; you'd be amazed at what you can buy fixtures for. Shop these stores several times a month, because the turnover in merchandise is awesome.

Wallpaper

While wallpaper really dresses up a house, doing the whole house can involve serious money. Remember the important rooms? Take the small ones, the bathrooms, and make them look great with wallpaper. It doesn't cost a lot and has great eye appeal.

Paneling

Don't panel the whole house, but look at key walls. You can make a difference by doing one wall in a room or doing a room in half paneling (lower half paneled and top half painted off-white).

The key is improvements that are visual and don't cost a great deal of money. You are looking for a property with the right things wrong with it.

WHAT NOT TO DO

You can avoid some mistakes by thinking ahead about what *not* to do.

Don't Buy What You Can't Fix

Beware of uncorrectable problems. Such problems might include a small bathroom in an older house that won't hold larger, modern fixtures and small bedrooms that won't hold modern-sized furniture.

Don't Make Major Repairs

Don't replace roofs, furnaces, air conditioning, wiring, and plumbing. These are structural improvements, not cosmetic improvements. You want to turn an ugly duckling into a beautiful swan, not do brain surgery. Leave rehabilitation of property to the pros, licensed contractors with experience in doing it. If you try to play amateur contractor, the subcontractors will eat you for breakfast. Don't get involved.

Don't Put on Additions

Don't add an extra bedroom or bath and try to make money on it. For the time and work you put in, you will get very little in return. Stick to the cosmetics. Don't put in a pool. It's a lot of hassle, and you'd be lucky to get your money back.

PACKAGE A PARTNERSHIP

From the investor whose hand doesn't fit hammers, you are about to learn there is a better way to go. Find a person who is good at fixing up. Get Carl the Carpenter and form a partnership. You will buy the property for little or nothing down and arrange a Title I loan or home improvement loan from the bank for the fix-up money. Carl does the work, and you sell the property and split the profit.

If you find yourself with some spare time, don't limit yourself to one Carl. You can get a Carl II or a Carla and make the same arrangement. They don't have to know about each other. You can make a lot of money in real estate by just learning how to package.

CHAPTER SEVENTEEN

Negotiation: A Learnable Art

A young couple who had been house hunting for several weeks finally found what they had been looking for. While touring with the seller, they could hardly contain themselves. The wife said, "Oh, honey, look at this kitchen, it's just perfect." The husband, observing the den, said, "My desk would fit perfectly right in that corner." They not only liked the other rooms, but they raved about the backyard being perfect for their child. They sat down with the seller and agreed to buy the house. Later, on the drive home, the husband said, "I really like the house, but it's too bad we couldn't get him to cut his price."

This is an extreme example, but how many of you are guilty of milder versions of it? Praising the property and then wondering why the price was so firm. Giving away your position, the emotional involvement, and watching a soft seller get hard before your very eyes.

Now take a different version of the story. A wise young couple approaches the same house. Although it is exactly what they are looking for, they remain poker-faced for the seller. They indicate their liking by squeezing hands. After this signal, they go defect hunting. Unless the kitchen is the size of the Los Angeles Rams' practice field, the wife says, "Is this all the kitchen?" Then, glancing at a stain on the ceiling, she adds, "How many times has the roof leaked?" The husband, looking at a discolored spot, says, "Are all the rugs stained this badly?" This goes on throughout the house. The yard is not quite right, either. It's either too small or there's a lack of privacy.

Coming back in the house, the husband says to the seller, "Let's sit down. We have another house to look at, but we do have a few minutes." After they're all seated, the wife says, "With all these defects, there is no way we could pay $75,000 [the asking price] for this house." They are then quiet and let the seller speak. The seller suggests he might take $70,000. The husband replies, "No, I don't think so." The seller says, "Well, what would you pay?" The husband replies, "With all these problems, what is the absolute minimum price you would sell this house for?" The seller finally admits he would take $65,000. The young couple made $10,000 in 10 minutes sitting at a table, and they got a home they absolutely loved. You have just learned the prime rule of negotiation:

HE WHO CARES LESS WINS

You cannot violate that rule. If you are going to win, you must at least appear to care less. Think of that before you start to negotiate next time. You negotiate several times a day whether you realize it or not. When you're negotiating with your kids, you trade a promise to finish their homework first for permission to play with their friends. For a couple of days, make a note of every time you negotiate— the number will amaze you. The simple fact of focusing and paying attention can make you a much better negotiator.

TEN TIPS

Here are 10 tips that should make you a better real estate negotiator.

Tip 1: Determine the Price

The old adage that the first person to mention a price loses has a lot of truth to it. During negotiating, get in the habit of answering a question with a question. When you're answering a question, you're on the defensive; when you're asking a question, you're on the offensive. If the seller says, "What would you pay?" you say, "What would you sell for?"

Keep your level of awareness high; don't let your mind wander. I use a little trick of a mild gasp when they first mention price, followed by a question: "Uuuh, how did you arrive at the price?" Right away you have them both defending the price and wondering whether they did set it too high.

Tip 2: Point Out the Defects

Always, during your inspection, point out what's wrong with the property, not what's right with it. We are trying to reduce the value in the seller's mind, not raise it. If you find yourself admiring the building, snap yourself back by saying to yourself mentally, "Let's see what else is wrong with it." It's important that you don't point out the defects belligerently. You don't want to offend the seller or make him or her mad. It's better to direct the seller's attention to the defect in the form of a mild question—not, *"What's that?!"*

Tip 3: Don't Give Away Your Position

No matter how much you want it, how soon you have to

have it—even if you feel your life will be changed forever if you don't have it—don't let the seller know it. Always let the seller know there is competition for your investment dollar. For example, say, "I'm looking at a few properties, and I'm definitely going to buy one of them."

Don't appear at all to be excited about this property, because if you do, you can end up paying 5 to 10 percent more for it than you had to. On a $100,000 property, that's $5,000 or $10,000. It's expensive to show emotion. Hold yourself in check.

Tip 4: What the Seller Says and What the Seller Means

The best negotiators in the world are great listeners. While the seller is talking, don't be thinking about what you're going to say next; tune in. The difference between "I'm asking $80,000" and "I'm going to get $80,000" is significant. The first one indicates flexibility, and the second doesn't. We're back to focus when you negotiate. A little training in this area, and you will do it automatically.

Tip 5: Make Small Concessions

Making small concessions in the early part of the nego- tiation process gives you two benefits. First, it helps the process flow more smoothly, and second, it obligates the seller when you get to major issues. (You've given up some things, now it's the seller's turn.) An example would be to agree to pay an inspection fee of, say, $100; in return you get the seller to lower the down payment requirement a few thousand. You pay an appraisal fee of $150 and ask for a price reduction. Be tough as nails on big concessions. Make the seller really work for any you give up, and always get something in return. "Well, I'm willing to do that if you'll ———."

Tip 6: The 6 Percent Solution

If a property is priced much more than you want to pay, the first counteroffer should indicate that the seller is flexible. I look for a 6 percent price reduction. As an example, let's look at the following numbers:

Asking price: $105,000
My planned purchase: $90,000
Initial offer: $80,000
Seller's initial counteroffer: $97,000

This is a potentially successful negotiation, since the seller's initial counter reduced the original asking price by more than 6 percent. The next couple of responses will let you know for sure.

Tip 7: Let the Seller Know When You're Close

In the example for Tip 6, if your maximum price is $90,000 and you first bid $80,000 and then jump to $90,000, you haven't conveyed to the seller what you want to convey. For all the seller knows, you would be willing to pay $95,000.

The best trainers in the negotiating business say the best negotiators concede in small increments. If, instead of jumping from $80,000 to $90,000, you countered with $85,000, then $87,000, then $88,000, you would let the seller know you were approaching the maximum you were willing to pay.

Tip 8: Give Yourself Room

Always give yourself room to negotiate. Never offer originally what you are willing to pay. I've always told my students, "What if they accept your original offer? You'll never know for the rest of your life what they really would have taken." If your first offer is accepted, you know you paid too much for the property.

In the example, although you were willing to pay $90,000, you offered only $80,000. Why not offer $50,000? Well, it's less than half the asking price. If you insult the seller, you will make him or her mad, and probably no negotiations will take place. The seller will just reject your offer outright, and you will be in the position (if you want the property) of making a second, higher offer even though the seller hasn't responded. That is a weak position from which to negotiate.

Tip 9: Give Price and Take Away Interest

Interest on a mortgage the seller is carrying back is a very strange thing. I have seen many sellers who are very firm on price and yet willing, very easily, to drop the interest rate on their mortgage. Interest rate to a seller is a lot like credit cards. People tend not to pay attention or negotiate when they're buying something with plastic, but they pay a lot more attention when buying with cash.

Interest, like plastic, seems to be "funny money." Somehow it's not real. This can work to your advantage. Take an example: Your offer for a property is up to $76,000, and the seller is standing firm at $78,000. He has agreed to carry back a $50,000 mortgage for 15 years at 10 percent interest. You say, "Okay, I'll go to $78,000 if you'll take 9 percent on your second mortgage." The seller readily agrees. What's the difference? The interest he gave away on that mortgage over the 15-year period is $5,531. Not a bad trade-off. It's even better if you can get the seller to take the extra $2,000 by increasing his mortgage to $52,000.

Tip 10: Break Down the Property

When you're buying property, it's a good idea to assign an actual value to the land and the building. Remember, you can only depreciate the building, not the land. The higher the value of the building, the more you can write off as depreciation. On your tax return you can probably get away with 15 percent land value. If you want a greater building-to-land ratio, make sure it says so on the contract. When you buy commercial property where the land has a greater value, this is even more critical.

TURN 10 PERCENT DOWN INTO VERY LITTLE DOWN

In the newspaper classified ads, you will often see an ad that says, "Only 10% down payment." In many cases the seller is looking to cover the closing costs and pay the real estate commission. If you have found a property that has below-market rents (rent raises increase the price) or below-market price because of a slight defect, it is easy to raise the sales price of the building after you own it. The key is to buy it. If a property is for sale for $100,000 and you don't have the $10,000 down payment, you are not in good shape to make the profit. Or are you? Let's see how you might cut the cash requirement down.

Real Estate Commission

If the broker is a member of the multiple-listing service (MLS), his or her property is listed in the MLS book. This property can be sold by any MLS member. There is probably a 98 percent chance it will be sold by someone else, and the listing broker will only get half the commission. So in his or her mind, half the commission is gone.

If the broker is the listing agent, you might have some crank. You could say, "Ms. Broker, how would you like to keep the whole commission rather than half? If I buy directly from you, you will get it all. Instead of 3 percent, you would get 6 percent [if that's the rate in your area]. All you have to do is carry your commission as a mortgage instead of cash, and on top of you getting twice as much money, I'll pay you interest on the mortgage." You can easily get a broker's attention by pushing his or her greed button. That would eliminate 6 percent of the 10 percent down payment right there.

The Rents

Rents are paid in advance and given to the buyer at closing. The best time to close is on the first or second of the month when you would get the rents paid back to you in cash. For instance, if you were to buy a six-unit building with each unit renting for $500, you would get $3,000 at the closing. This reduces the amount of cash you have to bring.

The Deposits

If you're in a state that doesn't require a trust account for deposits, these are refunded to you at closing. If the six-unit building had a $250 deposit for each unit, that's another $1,500 you don't have to come up with. You will find that, with a little planning, 10 percent down can mean very little down.

Melvin Megabucks and Barney Broke

Although you can build wealth in real estate starting with absolutely nothing (I know, because I did it), you may feel you need some help. You just can't bring yourself to go talk to people with nothing behind you and ask to buy their real estate. Well, that doesn't mean you can't do it; it just means you need to package yourself a little differently. What you don't have, someone else does.

Let's take a look at two individuals and how they might make a marriage that would be beneficial to both of them. This should give you some ideas about how you can package yourself.

MELVIN MEGABUCKS

Melvin has it made. He's a high-income doctor; he has an income of $100,000 a year; he is, to quote an old Southern expression, living high on the hog. He is driving a fancy car and lives in a great house in the best part of town.

163

Melvin only has two problems: He would like to pay less income tax (a solution that's available through the up-to-$25,000 exemption), and he would like to have even more income down the road (because it's being taxed at such low rates from 1988 on). He may have even read a couple of books on real estate investing and be convinced real estate is a great investment and probably the solution to his problems.

However, when he starts to think about tax shelter and extra income, some obstacles come to mind. First, Melvin is really not that motivated to go out, beat the bushes, and make it happen. He's living well, and he's just a little lazy because of that. Second, Melvin cherishes his weekends. He plays golf with the boys down at the country club, or he goes to the football game with friends, and he just doesn't want to change that routine. Third, there is a high correlation between six-figure incomes and sixty- to seventy-hour work weeks. Melvin's wife, Mary Megabucks, has said, "Melvin, if you spend one more hour away from me and the kids, you and I are going to get subdivided [a real estate term for getting divorced]."

Melvin has figured out he had better not go out eight or ten more hours a week and play real estate investor. He would love to have tax shelter now and some extra income in the future (real estate is tailor-made for this). He is just not sure how to go about it.

BARNEY BROKE

Barney is really in bad shape. He has virtually no cash, he has a low-paying job, and, because of long years at low wages, his credit report is probably not in good shape. Barney has one thing going for him. He has a burning desire to build wealth. He is one horse who has become thirsty. He has reached the moment in his life where one realizes that if financial independence is ever going to happen, one has to make it happen. His wife, Barbara

Broke, is behind him and is willing to pitch in and make it happen. Barney and Barbara are willing to work the newspaper ads, call sellers, chase down the good buys, write offers—in other words, do all the work. What's holding them back, they think, is a lack of financial backing.

Now, here we have an ideal marriage. Each would-be investor brings to the party what the other lacks. Melvin brings a large financial statement and good credit while Barney brings the willingness to find and write offers on property they can buy. What if Melvin doesn't like the property Barney finds? The chapter about writing the offer described escape clauses. Barney could add a clause that says "subject to partner's approval."

FINDING MELVIN

How does Barney find Melvin? Although Melvin needs Barney just as badly as Barney needs him, it is highly unlikely Melvin will go searching for him. (He can't work it into his schedule.) But no matter who you are socially or economically, you have some interface with people in higher-income groups. You go to see doctors, attorneys, dentists, or other businesspeople.

Please do not, while you're sitting there, say, "Would you like to buy a piece of real estate?" You give the impression you're trying to sell them something, and you will make them instantly defensive. A great opening line would be, "Do you know anyone who could use some tax shelter now and some large extra income down the road?" You will probably hear one of three answers:

1. Your prospect may say, "What do you mean?" You say, "Just that. Do you know anyone who wants to reduce taxes on a large income and make some large profits down the road?"
2. You may get a curt response like "No" or "I'm not

interested." In that case, you drop the subject and ask someone else.

3. You may get an interested response, something on the order of, "I do."

At this time, to take control of the situation, you could use a great sales technique called "takeaway." It's a version of playing hard to get. You might say something like, "No, I wasn't thinking about you, John. I wanted to know if you had a friend or associate who might be interested." He may ask, "What's the matter, isn't it good?" You say, "It's a great investment; do you know anybody who might be interested?" The key here is to make it difficult (but not too difficult) to have you think of him as the investor. You finally agree to talk to him about it.

Again, to maintain control, under no circumstances talk to your potential investor about it in his or her office during normal business hours. Set an appointment in his or her home or in the office *after* business hours are over. If you have to give a hint, say, "I've discovered a way we can work together and both make a lot of money. I'll talk to you about it tonight." When you're sitting down together, you could sweeten the offer by offering to take care of most of the management problems, so he or she wouldn't have to be bothered. For a busy Melvin, this is music to his ears.

ANOTHER WAY TO PACKAGE

Say the property has a breakeven cash flow, and Melvin needs all the available tax shelter from the building. Barney, being low-waged, has almost no need for tax shelter and can see a large profit from selling the building. Barney might allow title to be taken 99 percent Melvin and 1 percent Barney. Barney would retain an option to buy 49 percent of the building at the original price and terms. This would give Melvin almost double the tax shelter (which he needs), and Barney would still retain his profit down the road.

If you package in this manner, you should get the help of a good real estate attorney to draw up the documents. Down the road, at the time of option execution or sale, you will consider these dollars well spent.

THE LIFE OF THE RELATIONSHIP

The relationship is based on need and will end when the need is no longer there for both parties. As he builds a net worth and the confidence that goes along with it, Barney will need Melvin less and less. When Barney finds a no-down-payment situation and it's a property he can buy on his own, he should do it. He brings in Melvin only when he needs him. Melvin, on the other hand, is free to have more than one Barney. He may even ask Barney if he has any friends who would like to do the same thing.

To the Melvins of the world, I would suggest you run an ad in the paper for potential Barneys. You can make a lot of money with little effort. A good place to run it might be in the Real Estate for Sale column. Anyone reading it there would have the kind of desire you are looking for.

There are more ways to make money in real estate than I could cover in 10 books. There are so many ways to package a profit, and there is no excuse for just doing nothing. Whether you're Barney or Melvin, decide to treat the other person fairly. No long-term relationship can be based on anything else. Remember, greed is the greatest killer of profit. As a wise sage once said, "Fifty percent of something is worth a whole lot more than 100 percent of nothing."

CHAPTER NINETEEN

Gifts from the Government

The function of the Department of Housing and Urban Development (HUD) is to provide for sound development of the nation's communities and metropolitan areas. HUD works in the following areas:

- Community planning and development
- Housing
- Research and technology
- Fair housing and equal opportunity
- Consumer and regulatory functions
- Other insurance programs
- Disaster assistance

Trying to cover HUD in one chapter of a book would be like condensing *Gone with the Wind* into one paragraph. This chapter covers just one of the many HUD housing programs.

THE SECTION 8 MODERATE REHAB PROGRAM

The Section 8 Moderate Rehab Program is basically designed to rehabilitate rental units that are now substandard or have various building components that need repair or replacement. It does this by providing a rental income to the owner that will repay him or her for the rehabilitation costs, make it possible to meet the monthly expenses, and to also get a return on the owner's investment capital in the building. It provides rent subsidies to the elderly, handicapped, disabled, and lower-income families who otherwise could not afford decent housing.

THE WORKING PROCESS

Several steps are involved in this program. This discussion walks you through the process.

The Announcement

The housing authority announces, through public advertising, that it is accepting proposals for housing rehabs.

The Selection

The staff at the housing authority examines your project. To qualify for the program, each unit must require at least $1,000 of rehabbing. The staff looks at the feasibility of the proposal, taking into consideration rents, available financing, and cost of improvements. Whether the building is fully assisted or only partially assisted depends on the eligibility of the existing tenants.

The Assistance

If you are selected, and before the rehab work is done, the housing authority staff will assist you in getting financing and even help you select a contractor. They also help do write-ups on the work that needs to be done.

Before construction begins, the owner and the authority execute an agreement that says the building will be put under a Housing Assistance Payments (HAP) contract upon completion of the repairs. The agreement and the contract make getting the financing a lot easier, since any lender knows that most of the rent is paid by the government and that the low actual rent payment from the tenant creates a waiting list.

The Rehab

At this stage, the various contractors do the physical work on the property.

The Contract

The owner and the authority sign a 15-year contract. The contract states rents for the units, obligates the authority to pay a rent subsidy, and details the responsibilities of the owner and the authority.

Renting

The initial occupant can be either the current tenant or, if the unit is vacant, a tenant the owner selects from the authority's waiting list. As tenants without assistance leave the building, the owner selects new ones from the available list.

Rent Payments

The owner is paid 75 percent of the established rent directly from the government. The tenants pay the remaining 25 percent to the owner. Since a family is renting an apartment at 25 percent of market, they are normally quite willing to pay the landlord.

IS IT EASY?

Is it as easy as it sounds? No. You're dealing with the government and all that implies: delays, rejections, and sometimes a total absence of logic. You've got competitors, with other buildings, who compete with you for the money. If you've got the temperament to handle all of that, there is money to be made. Spend part of a day at your regional HUD office inquiring about the various programs. Some of them involve loans with very low interest rates.

CHAPTER TWENTY

How Much Should I Pay?

"Value is in the eye of the beholder" should be applied to the price put on some pieces of real estate. When you ask some people how they arrived at a price they say, "Uncle Charlie says it's worth that." Others use PFA (picked from air) as a scientific evaluation. Getting an appraisal is an accepted way to determine value, but this can have some holes in it.

An appraisal is an estimate of value by a human being who is not infallible. I've seen two appraisals vary by thousands of dollars. There are many types of appraisers, and they vary in expertise and accuracy. The most respected professional designation is MAI (Member Appraisal Institute). When lending institutions (banks and savings and loan associations) obtain appraisals for the purpose of loans, they require MAI appraisers.

After a while, it won't be necessary for you to get every property appraised before you buy it. You will learn your marketplace, as I did, and find you become a pretty good estimator of value. The discussion in this chapter is limited to residential property (single-family homes and apartment buildings) because that's what you should be buying right now. In the next few years, rental shortages, which have appeared in many cities (there are exceptions), should drive up rents and take prices right along with them.

THE TWO AREAS

Residential appraisals are of two basic kinds of property, divided according to the number of units in the building.

One to Four Units

The first category of appraisals includes single-family homes up to fourplexes. This is a unique group of property because it is normally appraised without regard to income stream. They are appraised mainly on the basis of comparable sales (comps). This means houses can be priced well beyond their ability to carry themselves as a rental property.

Duplexes and fourplexes have an additional problem. Everyone has heard that if you want to get started in real estate, you should start by buying a duplex or fourplex. Since most people follow the herd, they are out there buying them. That creates about five buyers for one seller in these properties, and following the basic laws of supply and demand, prices shoot up. If you're going to buy apartment buildings, avoid those with two or four units. Buy five units and up. If you look in a Real Estate for Sale column of an average newspaper, you find four-unit buildings priced at close to eight-unit buildings, and the eight-unit building has twice as much rent coming in. There is one exception: Take anything that's a steal. If you find an underpriced fourplex, buy it. You don't have to keep it; you can turn around and sell it on soft terms, taking your profit partly in cash and partly in paper (mortgage).

Five Units and Up

Buildings with five or more units tend to be appraised on the basis of income stream and tend to be much more sensibly priced than duplexes and fourplexes.

DETERMINING VALUE

Here's how value is determined with each kind of residential appraisal.

One to Four Units

Determining value with the single-family homes up through fourplexes is done mainly with comps. The appraiser needs access to other sales in the neighborhood. One source is the real estate brokerage houses. Anyone who belongs to the multiple-listing service (MLS) will do. This group shares listings through the publication of an MLS book (showing all the properties the group has for sale). This book shows asking prices, not selling prices. They also, as a part of the service, have a Sold book. This book lists all the group's current properties that have been sold and what they sold for. Appraisers depend on this book when they appraise a property.

Wouldn't this be a nice book to look in? Well, don't run into a real estate office and say, "Give me your Sold book." You're going to meet some resistance. Walk in and say, "I'm interested in buying some single-family homes and small apartment buildings here. Do you mind if I look at your Sold book to get an idea what property is selling for?" How many agents throw potential buyers out the door? Not many bright ones. If they hassle you, walk down the block to the next office and repeat the question. It won't take you long to find one.

Take a look at three-bedroom, two-bath (a great rental) sales in your area. In 10 or 15 minutes you will have a good idea of sales prices in your neighborhood. Some of these agencies are tied to a computer system, and they can run you off a page or two for reference. Obviously, if you don't start writing offers through the agent, your source will dry up quickly. With a few hundred offices in a good-sized city, that doesn't present much of a problem.

Comp sales of duplexes and fourplexes are listed in this book also. This exercise is important. You can't recognize wholesale if you don't know what retail is. You need to be able to spot a bargain.

Five Units and Up

Properties with five or more units are more likely valued based on the income stream, although there seem to be many ways to value income property. Many amateur investors make the mistake of using rules of thumb as evaluators. One of the most popular is some multiple of the gross income (something times the gross income). You hear these people say, "I buy buildings in this neighborhood at eight times or ten times the gross," or whatever it happens to be.

The problem is that this is a poor way to determine the value of a building because expenses can vary drastically on a property-by-property basis. Take utilities, for instance. The net income of a building can plummet depending on whether the tenants pay utilities or not. This can affect the value of the building a great deal.

Buy buildings where the tenants pay their utilities. They don't tend to conserve when you're paying the bill. Regardless, when you're buying a property, get 12 consecutive months of utility bills. Don't settle for 10 months and call that 10/12 of the bill. If you're missing January and February in Buffalo, New York, or July and August in Phoenix, you're in for a nasty surprise. Don't settle for the IRS form showing the seller's expenses. In anticipation of selling, the seller might have deferred paying the November and December bills until January, thereby reducing the apparent bill.

A more professional way of evaluating the property would be the *cap rate.* This is an abbreviation for "capitalization rate," which is a measure of how fast your investment capital is returned. Before you can understand that, you have to understand something called net operating income (NOI). This is the income of the building that remains after you pay all the expenses and before you pay the debt service.

Take the example illustrated in Figure 20A. You find a $250,000 building for sale. It has five two-bedroom apartments that rent for $700 per month. If you do a little multiplying, you will find that the maximum possible rent for the year is $42,000. The total expenses, including the property tax, are $14,900. You cannot assume that all the apartments will be occupied 100 percent of the time. People move out; you must clean the unit and then advertise for another tenant. You use a vacancy factor: You estimate that it will be 5 percent of the gross income (it may vary according to economic conditions). NOI is the $42,000 we start with, minus the 5 percent of the gross vacancy ($2,100) and minus the expenses ($14,900). The balance would be $25,000 (the NOI).

The cap rate is determined by dividing NOI by the price of the building:

$$\text{Cap rate} = \frac{\text{NOI}}{\text{Price of building}}$$

In the example, the cap rate would be:

$$\text{Cap rate} = \frac{\$25,000}{\$250,000} = 0.1, \text{ or } 10\%$$

If a 10 percent cap rate is good for your area and you buy a building at 11 percent (building price is less than $250,000), you have a good buy. If you buy one at 9 percent

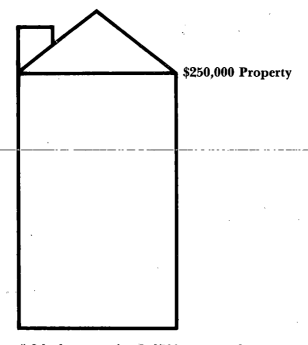

$250,000 Property

5 2-bedroom units @ $700 per month

Gross rent = $700 × 5 units × 12 months = $42,000

Vacancy factor = 5% × $42,000 = $2,100

Expenses (from income/expense sheet) = $14,900

Figure 20A

(building price of more than $250,000), you paid a little too much and should have gotten concessions on terms.

What's the cap rate in your area? I haven't the foggiest idea. They vary from area to area and neighborhood to neighborhood. You have to find out in your own market-place. Ask other investors and income-property brokers. It won't be long before you have a good feel for it.

A FEEL OF YOUR OWN

I, for one, am not that tied up on price if I can get soft terms (low-interest seller-carryback financing and low monthly payments). I know that 10, 15, or 20 years from now when that property has doubled or tripled in value, it won't matter that I paid a thousand or two too much for it. Use the previous guidelines in this chapter to determine whether you're in the ballpark of value, but don't get totally hung up on price if the seller is willing to work with you. Get a feel of your own.

THE FLY IN THE OINTMENT

When you're buying apartment buildings, you need to get accurate information about expenses. The income/ expense sheet given to you by the broker is a seller's sheet, not a broker's sheet. You may notice that down at the bottom of the page the broker says he or she doesn't guarantee it.

There are some ways to protect yourself:

- Have the seller warrant the expenses as being true and accurate. If they aren't, you have a good case for litigation.
- Get the past three years of the page for this property on the seller's tax return. The seller can't slip expenses over into another year if you get more than one year.
- Talk to the seller's tax adviser. This person is unlikely to lie and jeopardize his or her license, so you'll probably get the truth. Find out if the adviser is a relative and, if so, take your information with a grain of salt.

Estimating value is composed of a combination of knowledge and common sense. It won't take long to get it. Remember to concentrate on your farm area.

CHAPTER TWENTY-ONE

Management Money Makers

The key to hassle-free management is getting good tenants. Amateur landlording is expensive. Many beginners qualify tenants visually: "They were such a nice-looking couple; I can't believe they tore up my rental." Knowing that many people qualify visually, what do you think flakes, deadbeats, and property destroyers wear when they come to you front door? Old clothes? No—they're dressed to kill. Beware of overdressed people.

EVALUATING TENANTS

How can you evaluate prospective tenants? You can start with the three precautions described here.

Rental Application

Have them complete a rental application form. Verify their employment. If they haven't been at their current job long, find out how long they worked at their last one. Job skippers don't stay long, and they normally don't treat your property well, either. Also, if their rent is half of their total income, you're going to have a hard time collecting rent. It should be more in the range of 30 to 35 percent. Join your local apartment owner's association and ask for a good rental application form.

Credit Check

Run a credit check. If the prospects have a history of paying their bills, they will probably pay their rent. There's a clue: People who move in, don't pay any more rent, and then fight you tooth and nail to avoid leaving don't have good credit reports. You can weed out the flakes and deadbeats. Joining your local apartment owner's association should give you cheap access to the credit bureau.

Spot Visit

Make an unannounced spot visit. Stop by their current apartment the next afternoon before dark. When they answer the door, hold up the rental application form and say, "There's something here I didn't quite understand; could I come in for one moment?" If they refuse to let you in, that's a clue.

As soon as you step inside, tell them the bathroom story: "Could you help me out? I've been driving around for several hours, and I've got to use the bathroom." This lets you walk into the back of the house, perhaps glance into the bedrooms, and get a good look at it. I remember one check in my early days where I found a motorcycle parked in the living room with a dried pool of oil on the rug. I said, "What an interesting place to park a motorcycle." The guy said, "Yes, I'm so afraid it's going to be stolen that I park it inside." Needless to say, I didn't rent to them.

All of this doesn't mean you only rent to Carolyn Clean.

A little untidiness is OK, although the apartment shouldn't look like the Third Army bivouacked there. I'm looking for these problems:

- *Strong Odors*—The smell shouldn't knock you down when you walk in the door. There are people who leave soiled diapers laying around and don't carry out garbage. I know there are, because I've found them.
- *Signs of Damage*—Look for damage like holes punched in walls, cigarette burns, and anything else that costs money to fix.
- *Anything Out of the Ordinary*—You don't want a mad scientist who does chemical experiments in your apartment. You don't want to be awakened by a great explosion late one night and find yourself wondering if it's your building.

Common sense will help you out a lot in property management. You will develop, with practice, a little ability to read people.

TEN POINTS TO PONDER

Before you embark on a property-management scheme, ponder the following 10 points.

1. Single-family homes and small apartment buildings don't have tenant strikes.
2. Respond to tenants' complaints and fix things quickly. This can greatly reduce your tenant turnover.
3. Clean and (if necessary) paint a rental before you start to show it; otherwise you're wasting your ad dollars. Tenants can't visualize the finished product very well. If you're doing a fixer-upper building, paint and clean the outside first. You can then do the

inside apartments, one by one, and rent each as you finish it. Prospective tenants can't see inside the dirty units.

4. Keep your rents at market by shopping your competition several times a year. Don't try to get every last dime out of your tenants. If you try to play Scrooge, it will cost you money. The tenants will leave. Turnover is a major expense.

5. If you have a lot of vacancies, consider a specialty building. Look in the For Rent ads and see who's not being provided for. Senior citizens, cat lovers (charge a little more rent and get a large deposit), and women with small children (consider a bus service to a nearby child care center—and charge more rent, of course).

6. Instead of charging a late fee, give a discount on rent, say $100. (Mark it up above market and discount down to market.) Nobody will pay late. Bonuses of this arrangement are that you can evict for nonpayment of rent, usually not for nonpayment of late fees (the $100 is rent), and if rent control is voted in, you don't raise your rent, you lower your discount.

7. Make a damage list that you and the tenant sign before he or she moves in.

8. Regardless of the move-in date, prorate all rents to the first of the month. It makes bookkeeping easier.

9. Check out the tenants before they move in. If you live in a state in which the laws favor tenants, getting them out can be very difficult.

10. Don't let tenants get two months behind. If they can't afford one month's rent, they sure can't afford two months' rent. Serve late notices and eviction notices promptly.

CHAPTER TWENTY-TWO

How to Crank the Bank

Contrary to popular opinion, banks are in the business of lending money. They want to lend money, since they have money in the bank they are paying rent (interest) on, and they want to get it out at a higher interest rate than they are paying. The difference is called profit (music to a banker's ears).

Banks prefer not to lend money to people who truly need money; they would much rather lend it to people who don't need money. One of the worst things to say to a banker is, "I don't need it." It has the psychic effect of a punch in the nose. Statements like, "That much would handle it," or, "It's a good loan so I brought it to you first," are much, much better.

The other thing a banker looks at is repayment. You would think, since it's not the loan officer's money, he or she would be less finicky. It's not that at all—it's a matter of job security. The fastest way to become an ex-banker is to make loans that people don't pay back. A nice statement to drop is, "The nice thing about this loan is the ease with which I can pay it back." The banker won't kiss your hand, but it won't go unnoticed.

ESTABLISHING THE RELATIONSHIP

Never walk into a bank unannounced and open an account. In the banker's mind, that puts you in the category of the great unwashed. Come in by appointment, and come in by referral. If you're new in town, how do you get a referral? If you have a job, you have a referral. Talk to your bookkeeper at work and find out where the company banks. Call the banker and make an appointment. You might say, "This is [your name] with the Jones Company. Charlie Smith, our comptroller, speaks highly of you, and I would like to come down, open an account, and discuss my banking needs with you."

On the first meeting, never talk about taking money out. That comes later. Talk about the money you'll be putting in. You're going to be buying some real estate, so you could say, "I'll be buying some real estate shortly, and I'll open the property accounts here." (Even though your net cash flow may be next to nothing, the process of collecting rents and paying bills on a small building creates a large cash flow through the bank account.) I opened an account on a 15,000-square-foot office building at one bank, and they sent me an American Express Gold Card and a $2,000 line of credit I hadn't asked for, even though I lived in a different state.

A little side note on lunches: If you go to lunch with a banker, never pick up the check. The one who pickcd up the check got the most out of the meeting, and you want that to be the banker. If the paper turns brown with age, don't pick it up. If spider webs form, don't pick it up. If it goes on forever, say, "Why don't I take you out later when it's not business, and I'll pick it up then." The banker will get the idea.

BORROWING WITH BAD OR NO CREDIT

Will a banker lend you money if you have poor or no credit? Usually yes, if you eliminate the bank's risk. How could you do that? You could if you had the money to repay the loan in the bank at the time you took out the loan. You could put $1,000 into a bank, pledge it as collateral for a $1,000 loan, and pay the loan back better than agreed (get a payment or two ahead). Wouldn't that be a great credit reference? If you did it with three banks, you'd have three credit references. When you fill out any loan application form, they always ask for three credit references. Get the idea? It's a great way to rebuild credit.

If the banker asks, "Why do you want the loan?" never lie. The banker will find out via your credit report. Say, "I don't really need the money. I've had credit problems in the past, and I want to rebuild my credit. I'm going to borrow this money from you and pay it back promptly, so you'll give me a good credit reference."

A word of caution: Get an installment loan, not a commercial loan. An installment loan is one you make principal and interest payments on, and they're longer than 120 days. You might get a six-month loan to be on the safe side. Commercial loans don't appear on your credit report. The borrowing arrangement with the three banks could cost you about $200 in interest (depending on rates). But remember—you aren't in it for a profit, you're "buying" three great credit references.

HOW ABOUT A CREDIT CARD?

You would get a credit card the same way. Put $500 in a certificate of deposit, and pledge it as collateral for a $500-limit Visa or MasterCard. Do banks to that? All the time. Have you ever seen those funny little ads that say, "You can get a credit card with bad credit"? They charge you a stiff fee, and all they do is set up a bank where you can get a card backed by your CD. You don't need them; you can do it yourself.

Did you notice something about department stores? Many of them will grant you a credit card if you have a valid Visa or MasterCard. Use your newly acquired card to get store cards. Charge something you need and pay promptly. They all report to the credit bureau, and you can easily start to rebuild your credit.

THE CREDIT BUREAU

Changes in the federal law now protect you from faulty credit reporting. It's a good idea to get a copy of your credit report twice a year and check it for wrong entries. You'll pay a fee of about $10. If you have been refused credit within the last 30 days, the people you applied to have to give you a copy free. It's the law.

Here are two other things you can do:

1. For every bad mark on your credit report, you are entitled to include an explanation of your side of the story. If you had a problem and cleared it up, tell your side. They have to include it with any credit report they send out on you.
2. If you disagree with anything in the report, you can have the credit bureau write to the questionable source for an explanation. You may get the report modified with the response. If there is no response after a given number of days, the item is removed from your credit report. In this land of many lawsuits, people sometimes choose not to respond to letters of this type.

Clean up your report as best you can, and get a good credit report in front of the bad credit (indicating your effort). You'll be surprised what you can borrow with a bankruptcy on your credit report, if there is some good credit sitting in front of it.

CHAPTER TWENTY-THREE

Ten Ways to Eliminate Negative Cash Flow

Negative cash flow is much more of a knowledge problem than it is a problem with the price of real estate. When you are dealing with a motivated seller with substantial equity in the property (I like at least 25 percent), you will find there are many ways to structure payments to reduce the negative. The reason I like the seller to have substantial equity is that the more equity he or she has, the greater the effect of lowering the payment to him or her on lowering the total payment on the property.

The following 10 ways are not the only ways to eliminate negative cash flow; there are probably 30 or 40 ways at least. However, these will get your mind working and give you some options. When you know your options and are blessed with common sense, you can sit down with a seller and put a transaction together.

THE MORATORIUM

"Moratorium" literally means no payments. Although you do owe the seller money, you are making no payments on the mortgage—neither principal nor interest. This could be done using either of two methods:

1. Make no payments for a shorter period of time, say a year, to give you time to raise rents and build up a cash reserve, and then a monthly payment would begin. A motivated seller might accept no payments for 6 to 12 months if he or she really wants to sell. Ask!
2. Make no payments for a longer period of time, say five years. You defer all payments to the seller—principal and interest—and then pay everything in the form of a balloon payment. This is much less attractive to the seller, and you need a stagnant marketplace or a "Get me out of here" attitude on the part of the seller.

Note: To the extent you are deferring interest to the seller, you are experiencing negative amortization. In other words, you will owe more when your loan comes due than the original value of the loan. That makes this technique much more attractive in an area of good appreciation and a history of good appreciation than in an area where appreciation is not very great. It's much better for a Sun Belt city than for a Buffalo, New York.

INTEREST-ONLY WITH BALLOON

The payment on a $100,000 15-year loan is $1,220.20 per month. An interest-only payment at the same interest rate is only $1,000 per month, a savings of $220.20 per month.

The difference between the two payments can sometimes do a lot to get rid of negative cash flow. Normally, with most seller financing, these interest-only loans are accompanied by a balloon payment (all due and payable). Unless you get serious concessions from the seller, don't accept a balloon payment in under five years. In the unstable money markets that exist today, you can create some serious problems for yourself.

INTEREST-ONLY WITH AMORTIZATION

I prefer an interest-only loan followed by amortization. You would pay only interest for a few years, and then the loan would be paid off with a number of higher equal monthly installments. For example, you could pay interest for 3 years, then a 15-year loan would kick in. You would get higher payments down the road when you had higher rents to make the payments with.

Get a mortgage payment book from an office supply store and familiarize yourself with the differences in the various payments. It will help you no end when you are writing offers.

SPLIT-INTEREST FUNDING

Take a $100,000 mortgage at 12 percent with an interest-only payment of $1,000 per month. Your problem is that the property can only carry $600 per month. The solution: You offer the seller part of the owed interest (say, $500 per month) as a payment, and you defer the remaining $500 per month for a period of five or six years and then have it due in a balloon payment. This will give you a positive cash flow of $100 per month, and any additional rent raises will put more positive cash flow in your pocket. This method is much more attractive to the seller, who gets some payment on his or her equity, so sellers are much more likely to accept it.

LEASE WITH OPTION TO BUY

Chapter 10 showed you how to put lease-options together. This works great in areas where prices have greatly outpaced rents. It lets you control homes in the more expensive area of town (where appreciation can make enormous profits), and yet keep your monthly payments down to a level where you can rent the property at a rent that brings a positive cash flow.

SELL A PERCENTAGE TO AN INVESTOR

High-income investors don't necessarily need cash flow; they could use some tax shelter now and additional income down the road. If you are willing to shoulder a large part of management (not all, because of the hands-on requirement of the new tax law), it's even more attractive to them. You could deed them an interest in the property in return for their making all the payments that make up the negative cash flow (which they can offset against other real estate income).

MAKE THE LOAN LONGER

The longer the loan in years, the lower the monthly payment. If you made the loan of the seller's equity, say, 40 years instead of 10 or 15 years, you would have a much lower monthly payment. To make this arrangement attractive to the seller, you may have to include a balloon mortgage at a negotiated time in the future. However, don't assume. My first mortgage was carried back by the seller for a period of 39½ years at a very low interest rate. I was really dumb about real estate when I first got started. I hadn't been told by all the "smart" people that a seller would never accept it, so I wrote the offer that way, and it was accepted. We can sometimes be too smart for our own good.

LET THE LENDER PARTICIPATE

Today loans are available in which the lender will lend you money at below-market interest rates. This can greatly reduce the amount of monthly payment for the loan. In return, the lender will take a percentage of the profits at the time the home is sold. This gives you a lower payment and lets the lender take a portion of his or her profit down the road (a much larger profit than the little more extra interest he or she would collect today).

An even greater motivation for the lender is that it makes tens of thousands more people eligible for a home loan (with the lower payment). This means the lender can make a lot more loans (more profit).

DISCOUNT A CURRENT MORTGAGE

When you get new financing on a property you are buying, you are normally cashing out existing mortgages. Especially with private mortgages, you have an opportunity to buy that paper at a discount for cash. You have information the mortgage holder does not—you know the loan is going to be paid off. This will put cash in your pocket.

This cash can be put in a holding account (perhaps a money market fund) and be used to service any negative cash flow on the property. It could give you a year or two of grace before you would have to feed the building. At that time you could sell, bring in a partner, or whatever.

LOWER THE INTEREST

When you are dealing with a motivated seller, you are dealing with two trade-offs—price and terms. If the seller names the price, you should get to name the terms. If you can negotiate a loan at a lower interest rate, say, 9 percent instead of 12 percent, you can greatly reduce your monthly payment whether you are paying interest only or amortizing the loan. This can do a lot to solve problems from negative cash flow.

The key is to communicate with the seller. Make some suggestions, and ask if he or she has any. You might write the offer three or four different ways and ask the seller which is best for him or her. Stop complaining that it won't work, and look around for ways to make it work.

Leave It to Your Family, Not to the Government

Thank God for small favors. The Economic Recovery Tax Act of 1981 made some long-needed changes to the law on estate taxes. These changes include:

- The maximum estate tax, even on larger estates, has been lowered to 50 percent. The old rates almost amounted to confiscation.
- By 1987, assets worth up to $600,000 can avoid estate tax. This change was sorely needed, since the original intention of Congress was that most estates be exempt. Unfortunately, since the original numbers were passed, inflation caused large to become small; the buying power of the dollar had diminished greatly.
- All assets may be left to the surviving spouse without paying any estate tax at all. This eliminated the devastation of surviving spouses, left with a business, being driven out of business by the estate taxes created by their spouse's death.

WHAT DO YOU NEED?

Although you might think none of this will ever mean much to you, following the principles in this book can build a sizable estate in just a few short years, triggering problems with estate taxes. If your estate is under $600,000, your main concern is to have a good will. (If you die without one, you aren't shafted; your heirs are.)

A problem occurs when the estate moves to over $600,000 in value. When you own a lot of real estate and it appreciates in value, you may pass through this barrier and not even notice it. When you get close, it becomes important to prepare, on a yearly basis, an estimate of net worth.

To see why that's important, consider an example of unnecessary estate tax being paid. A husband and wife have an estate worth $1 million. The husband dies and leaves everything to his wife. A few years later, she dies and leaves everything to the children. Since her estate can exempt only $600,000, it must pay inheritance tax on $400,000 ($1 million minus $600,000). The estate pays a tax bill of $135,000 that proper estate planning could have avoided.

What if, instead of leaving his assets to his wife, the husband had left them in trust for his children, with the wife getting the benefits (income) of the assets during her lifetime. His $500,000 passes to the children tax-free (up to $600,000 is exempt), and her $500,000 passes tax-free also. Spend a little money on a good tax-planning attorney and you can save a lot.

SOME OTHER IDEAS

Do advance planning. As an example, if you have a company that is growing rapidly, and you can see it will be worth a great deal down the road in a few years, plan now. A simple matter of dividing stock into preferred and common, and giving the common stock (highest potential for growth in value) to your heirs, could save enormous amounts of estate tax.

If your estate is large, start giving it to your heirs now. Under the new laws, you can give away $10,000 per year, per child, without triggering gift tax, and your spouse can do the same thing. Let's say you have three children. That means you and your spouse could give them $60,000 per year, $600,000 per decade, or $1.2 million over a period of 20 years (if they are minors, use a trust). Since this giving would come off the top of your estate (the part taxed at a 50 percent rate), you could give your children a dollar instead of your estate giving them 50 cents (less probate costs).

You can give even more. You are allowed under the law to pay tuition costs and medical expenses, above and beyond the $10,000 without triggering gift tax. A word of caution: This money must be paid directly to the school, hospital, or doctor, and not to your child (who would pay them).

A creative way to get your property outside of your estate (lower estate, lower probate costs and estate tax) would be to sell your property to your heirs and let them pay you, as compensation, a monthly or yearly annuity. To avoid IRS problems, the annuity should be based on life insurance actuary tables. When you die, the payments would stop, and there would be nothing left in your estate to be taxed. (If you sold by carrying a long-term note, the note would be left.)

You could sell your property to your child at the very lowest estimate of fair market value. Tell an appraiser you want the lowest price he or she can put on the property and still sleep nights. Sell it for no down payment and take an interest-only mortgage back for your equity. Each year you and your spouse forgive $20,000 of the principal of the mortgage until your equity is gone. The child owns it, and there is no estate tax.

If you have no heirs, or if you like them like dogs and cats, you may consider a charitable remainder trust. You donate your asset to your favorite charity, take a tax write-off in the year of the donation and more later, and the charity pays you an annuity for the rest of your life. This would stop at your death, and there would be nothing left to probate.

WHAT STATE ARE YOU IN?

As you start to build wealth, it starts to become important where your state tax home is. You may have reached this level and just haven't thought about it. Your business situation may allow you to live anywhere, and moving your tax home could have some distinct advantages.

For instance, Alaska, Florida, Nevada, South Dakota, Texas, Washington, and Wyoming have no state income tax. At the other end of the scale is Minnesota with a high state income tax rate of 16 percent. Many states have rates over 10 percent. You have to consider estate tax also. Texas, which has no personal income tax, takes a healthy bite when you pass on.

I don't live in Reno, Nevada, by accident. It's a great place to live, which is a fairly well-kept secret. It also has:

- No state income tax
- No state inheritance tax
- No corporate income tax
- No inventory tax

It is a great business climate. Reno was just named, by *Money* magazine, one of the 15 boom areas of the country over the next 15 years.

The information in this chapter is presented for idea purposes only; it is not designed to take the place of tax planning with an attorney who specializes in the field. If you don't plan, you will never know the damage you have caused. (You'll be gone.) Your children will bear the brunt of your shortsightedness. Since yesterday is a cancelled check and tomorrow is a promissory note, this is not something that you can, in good conscience, put off.

CHAPTER TWENTY-FIVE

Putting the Pros on Your Side

There's no requirement that you walk your path alone or do everything yourself. There are people in the business who can be very helpful. Don't hesitate to use them.

AGENT/BROKER

One good agent/broker is worth 25 bad ones. Unfortunately, real estate is not an industry flooded with great agents. Finding one will take some searching on your part. Look for a referral. Talk to friends, relatives, investors, title officers, and bankers. When you hear the same name several times, that's a potential agent for you. Don't just talk to them on the telephone. Call, make an appointment, and sit down face to face. Let them know you're serious. Only then will they start to work for you.

CPA

A good certified public accountant is a must before you get too far along in your investment program. When your return includes investment property, I would strongly suggest you don't use the roadside accounting firm. A good CPA is always free. He or she will save you more in taxes than you pay in fees.

ATTORNEY

Don't get just an attorney, but an attorney who specializes in real estate. You need a source to answer real estate questions you don't know the answers to and may need him or her for closings, depending on the state you live in.

To find one, work on referrals. A person who has done good work for others will, no doubt, do good work for you.

ESCROW/TITLE OFFICER

A competent escrow officer who can assist your title searches and do fast closings (with motivated sellers) is worth his or her weight in gold. I have found, on many occasions, the decision to sell me the property was made because of the offer of the quick closing. Find this person through referrals.

APPRAISER

A good appraiser is a necessity. There are occasions when you will need help determining value, and you need to know an appraiser who knows your name and can give you fast service when the situation demands it. Your local apartment owner's association or your banker can help you find one.

PROPERTY RENTAL COMPANIES

These are companies that charge a fee to prospective

tenants to give them a list of available rentals. They are, in many cases, free to the landlord. It just makes sense to list your property with them to get a free source of tenants. Find them in the Yellow Pages or in the classified ads of your newspaper.

PROPERTY INSPECTOR

A property inspector is a person who, for a fee of around $200, will inspect a home and, through a written report, inform you of any defects in the property. If you are a rank beginner and know nothing about property, it would be a good idea to use one for your first few properties. It is money well spent and is better than a nasty surprise after the closing. Your local real estate broker or banker can put you in touch with one.

FOOD FOR THOUGHT

A young investor, just getting started in real estate, presented an offer to an elderly property owner. It called for no cash down and very liberal payments on the seller's equity. The seller, after reading the offer said, "I'm not going to take it; it's just not good enough." The young man, wise beyond his years, said, "I can't really blame you; it's not a great offer. I'm young and trying to get started. Tell me, how did you get started?"

The old man's eyes softened as he started to think. He said, "When I was young, an old man gave me a break. He let me have his property, even though I was young and didn't have any money. I took that and built everything I own today. I hadn't thought about it for a long time, but I wonder what would have happened to me if he hadn't helped me." When he had finished speaking, the young man looked at him and said, "I can't think of a single reason why you should sell me this building except that I need a break." He got his building.

CHAPTER TWENTY-SIX

Tangible Tips

1. One of the great ways to keep bad tenants out of your property is to run a credit check. You eliminate flakes and deadbeats who get behind and make midnight moves or who move in, never pay another month's rent, and fight you tooth and nail when you try to evict them. To join the credit bureau for the purpose of checking out a few tenants is much too expensive. One solution is to join the local apartment owner's association. In most cases, membership will get you access to the credit bureau.

Another solution is a company called Tenantcheck. They are located at 51 Monroe Street, Suite 1506, Rockville, MD 20850. Their telephone number is 1-301-279-9080. For a small fee—$16 for three-day service, $20 for one-day service—they will verify a tenant's worthiness for you (employment income, rental history, etc.). If you approve the tenant, they will guarantee the lease. If the tenant skips, you get $500 or one month's rent, whichever is less. That's a lot of protection for a small fee.

2. What a savings and loan association recommends to you is not necessarily best for you. Reducing the length of your mortgage, while only increasing your payment a small amount, can save you enormous amounts of interest. For example, a $50,000 30-year mortgage at 12 percent interest would cost you a total of $135,152 in interest, and your payment would be $514.31 a month. A $50,000 15-year mortgage (at the same interest) would cost you a total of $58,014 in interest, and your payment would be $600.08 per month. For an increase of $85.77 a month on your payment, you would save $77,138 in interest.

3. If you can't afford the extra monthly payment on a shorter mortgage, here's another solution. Contact your lender and say you want to make your payments twice a month instead of once a month. In other words, you would pay one-half of your mortgage on the 15th of the month and one-half of the payment on the last day of the month.

What difference does that make? You're cutting down the compound interest by making half the payment two weeks early. To be more specific, a $50,000 mortgage at 12 percent interest would cost you $135,152 in interest if you paid it off once a month for 30 years. If you paid if off with payments twice a month, you would pay only $77,144 in interest, saving you $58,088. A whopping 43 percent of the interest would disappear and, if you paid twice a month, would help you budget your house payment. By the way, the loan would pay off in 19 years instead of 30. Not all lenders will let you make payments twice a month; check with yours.

4. If you have some spare cash and you want to earn maximum return between investments, you might like to know which banks are paying the highest yields. There is a service available for $84 per year which will give you the top 100 federally insured banks on a weekly basis. Order this from Robert K. Headly, 100 Highest Yields, P.O. Box 088888, North Palm Beach, FL 33408.

When you are deciding where to put your money, you might also ask the banks these questions:

- Does my interest start on receipt of funds or after my check clears?
- Do you have any other special rates? (Don't assume the service picked it up.)
- What is your penalty for early withdrawal [in case of emergency]? This varies from bank to bank.

5. Advertise yourself. Don't keep the fact you're a real estate investor hidden from the world. Tell everybody—friends, neighbors, and coworkers. If you have some spare cash, run a small classified ad in your local newspaper (especially if you've had some practice talking to sellers). Your phone will ring. Run a simple ad like:

I buy real estate
Hollis, 888-9999

6. If you are considering conventional financing, don't exclude mortgage brokers from your search. They have access to out-of-town lenders, who may have money to lend at lower rates than in-town lenders. It's certainly worth a few phone calls.

7. Use a free service. Check with your local title companies. There is normally one that publishes a weekly report on mortgage money. It contains many local lenders and mortgage bankers and the current available rates on their funds. It's a way to shop for money without leaving your living room.

8. Investigate Title I loans. Some banks, except in tight-money markets, make Title I loans. These are government-insured loans made for the specific purpose of fixing up property. They are made for a maximum of $15,000 on a single-family home. Apartment fix-up loans are also available. Check with your banker on availability, rates, and maximum amounts. Credit unions love to make Title I loans.

9. Achieve energy savings. As much as one-third of the energy bill on your home may be created by air leaks. A

simple job of caulking and weather-stripping could cut 10 percent off your bill. A circulating fan that can be reversed to pull heat down in winter and up in summer can be a big saver. A hot-water heater can save up to 20 percent of your bill. Most water heaters are set at 140°, which is not necessary unless your dishwasher lacks a superheating element. If it has one, you could lower the setting to 120° and save about 20 percent of what your hot-water heater is costing you. Wrapping the heater and its pipes with insulation can save even more.

10. If you are buying a home from a couple getting a divorce and they are very bitter, you may have a problem getting them to accept a common note and mortgage, since they don't want to have any contact with or remembrance of each other. Consider two notes, secured by a single mortgage, so they would each have their own individual note. A simple thing like that could put a transaction together. There are other uses for this idea; give it some thought.

11. Hire your kids. Allowances are not tax-deductible; wages are. There is work around property that children, except for very small ones, can do. Hire them and pay them a reasonable wage to mow lawns, pick up trash, paint, do minor repairs, and whatever. Because these salaries are a business expense, they are totally tax-deductible. You will also teach them about real estate and the value of money at the same time (check limits under the new tax law).

12. Bookkeeping is really not that hard. Office supply stores sell specialty books for various businesses. Buy the one for real estate and just fill in the blanks. If you've hired managers for your buildings, they will do it for you.

13. As you build wealth, be sure you are adequately protected by insurance. Some companies provide a blanket $1 million liability policy (on your rental houses and personal home) that acts a lot like major medical insurance. If a large lawsuit goes against you, it pays any overage of your regular insurance policy. The cost is $200 to $300 per year. State Farm has it, and you should compare prices with other companies in your state.

14. Larger estates should be further protected with living trusts. If you own properties in other than your own state of residence, put them into a trust to avoid lengthy and expensive probate, in case of your sudden demise.

15. Remember, the only security you'll ever have is the knowledge in your mind. It's not material possessions; these can all be taken from you. No one can take away your knowledge of how to create wealth.

16. If you're in your early 50s and you want to sell your home and get the over-55 exemption on tax, consider a lease with option to buy. Make the lease long enough to reach your 55th birthday before the option can be exercised. Since you must live in the house three of the last five years, the lease can be no longer than two years.

17. What you want to be worth tomorrow, you must be in debt today. A dollar in mortgage debt is a dollar in net worth when a property doubles in value. Whether it takes 8, or 10 or 12 or 15 years to happen, you only have to wait.

18. If you are buying an older home, you should look for many things during your inspection. You might order a copy of "Inspection Checklist for Older Homes" from: Inspection Checklist, The Old Home Journal, 69-A Seventh Avenue, Brooklyn, NY 11217. The price is 50 cents.

19. One of the things that can add thousands to the selling price of a house is trees. Plant them when you first buy. Years later, when you sell your home, they can raise the value quite a bit.

20. Never take short-term balloon mortgages, the one- to three-year variety. Get them in the seven- to ten-year range. You will have a lot more options available to you ten years from now due to appreciation than you will have in two or three years. These short-term loans are called short fuses because they blow up on you. I have also heard them called neutron loans, named after the bomb. They blow up, kill the people, and leave the real estate.

21. The residential replacement rule, Section 1034 of the Internal Revenue Code, allows you to generate some tax-free cash. You can sell your old home for all cash, buy

another house the same price or more for nothing down (100 percent financing), use the cash to invest, and still defer all your taxes. If you bought discounted mortgages (see Chapter 11) with 20 to 40 percent returns and paid 12 percent rent on the new loan money, you could make a nice profit.

22. If you buy a property using a wraparound mortgage, make sure the underlying mortgages will be paid. Arrange to make your payment to an escrow company or other neutral depository, and let them pay the underlying mortgages and send the balance to the seller. The few dollars for the service charge will buy you a lot of peace of mind. If the seller wants the extra return on his or her money generated by the wraparound mortgage, ask him or her to pay the service fee.

23. To justify the percentage of the purchase price you allocate to the building (in order to depreciate it), you might think of using the fire insurance agent's replacement cost. It's usually high and is acceptable to the IRS.

24. If you're considering getting an adjustable-rate mortgage (ARM) on your home, understand they are so risky most lenders won't put a second mortgage on your home if the first is an ARM. The only reason to use an ARM would be if you planned to sell the home in a year or two. It is fully assumable and would give you lower payments for that year or two.

25. When you are buying a home, look at window placement and electrical outlets. You should be able to place your furniture without blocking a window, and there should be an electrical outlet in the middle of each wall.

26. If you put up a deposit with your offer to purchase a piece of real estate, use a personal check. Put two stipulations in the offer: (1) The check is not to be cashed until the offer is accepted and all conditions of sale are removed. (2) The buyer is to be notified when the check is to be deposited. This will let you withhold the actual cash until you are reasonably sure there will be a closing, and it lets

you keep your money in a money market fund (drawing interest) until you must withdraw it to cover the check.

Your agent may tell you he or she must deposit all checks within three days. This state law normally is waived if the contract says otherwise. (Check with your attorney.) Remember to remind the real estate agent that a counteroffer is not an acceptance.

27. If you own a mortgage and you want to buy a home, don't discount the mortgage to raise cash. That could cost you thousands of dollars. Instead, offer the mortgage you own for the down payment on the house you're buying. If you have to, sweeten it a little by adding some cash to the down payment. A motivated seller could find this attractive.

28. Property tax and fire insurance impounds are required for mortgages involving the FHA, VA, savings and loan associations, and banks when the loan exceeds 80 percent of the appraised value of the property. Consider that your home may have appreciated since you bought it, and a new MAI appraisal may put your insurance under the 80 percent figure.

Getting pushy with your lender could get your impound account released. What's the benefit? The lender doesn't get the interest-free use of your money in advance of the payment.

29. If you are buying single-family homes and are not knowledgeable, you might consider using a professional property inspector. He or she will inspect and prepare a written report for about $200. It can save you a big surprise after closing. Your banker or real estate broker can put you in touch with one. One of your "out" clauses (see Chapter 5) would be "subject to buyer's approval of this report."

30. The Gart-St. Germain Act of 1982 prohibits a bank from enforcing a due-on-sale clause when one spouse of a divorcing couple transfers title to the other spouse. The same is true for estate planning, such as putting the property into a trust. This was brought about by lender abuses. From changes come opportunity. You could put

your property, with a due-on-sale clause mortgage, into a trust and, upon sale, just transfer the beneficiary of the trust instead of the house itself. Consult your real estate attorney.

31. When you buy a home, it's a good idea to rekey the locks, although many people don't do it. You don't know who has a key, and a forgotten brother, unaware of the sale, walking in at 1 A.M. could be a contributing cause of heart failure.

32. If you have an uncontrollable urge to pay off your mortgage early, write your lender and see if he or she will cut your interest rate in half if you double your mortgage payments (assuming you can afford it). Your lender should, because the yield will be increased (see Chapter 11). If you can raise your payment only 50 percent, ask the lender to reduce your interest by 25 percent.

33. Smoke detectors are valuable life-saving tools, not only for your own home, but for your rental houses also. (They not only save lives, but also the litigation resulting from a loss of life.) Some localities require them by law. Check with your fire insurance agent about getting a discount because you have installed smoke detectors. The discount could more than pay for the detectors.

34. When you are buying a house, ask yourself one question: How easily can I sell it? If you can't find a good answer, you might consider not buying it.

35. Don't get emotionally involved with real estate. Love means nothing in tennis and also in real estate. The only question to ask is, "Is it a good investment?" The one exception to that rule could be your own home. It is important that you don't make money just for the sake of making money. In case you haven't heard, there are no U-Hauls behind hearses. It's important that you enjoy the fruits of your labor. Live in the house you want to live in, even though it might not be the greatest investment you can find.

36. If you took a mortgage at a high interest rate when you bought a home and interest rates have dropped 3 percent, consider refinancing your home. You should be planning to live there for the next few years so you can realize a profit from the lower payments to offset the cost of refinancing.

37. A great many states have purchase-money laws. If a seller carries back a trust deed or mortgage as a part of the purchase price, no deficiency judgment is allowed in the event the house sells for less than the mortgage value at a foreclosure sale. Check with your real estate attorney about your state.

38. If you're over 55, make sure you've lived in your present home for three of the last five years when you sell it. You can get a $125,000 exemption on taxes. Talk to your tax adviser. For couples over 55 who are planning to marry, if you've used your exemption and you marry a person who hasn't, you take away your spouse's exemption. It may pay to sell a home before the wedding.

39. If you're buying real estate for resale, remember that very long grass (from an abandoned property) takes weeks to turn green and look good. Invest a few dollars and mow it before the closing. You can really speed up the resale process.

40. When selling a property, your ad should use zinger headlines that will cause people to call. The secret is to get a lot of people interested in looking at it. Use headlines like: "No Qualifying," "Move in Quick," "Low Down," or "Owner Financing."

41. Carry legal forms and deeds around in your briefcase. Know a notary who, for a fee, will come to a home to notarize a deed. You never know when a good deal will pop up.

42. Develop other investors as friends. They will reinforce your program and keep you on track. When you are choosing a CPA, attorney, or real estate broker, a good

question to ask is, "How much did you pay in income taxes last year?" This tells you a lot about the other person's goals and motivations.

43. Print a flyer and pass it out through the neighborhood. It should indicate that you both buy and sell houses (if you do). Indicate that owner financing is available, and it's easy to qualify.

44. Advise your tenants to get tenant insurance. It protects their belongings and only costs about $100 per year. Shop agents and give tenants the numbers of the cheapest ones. Pass out a flyer along with your rental agreement.

45. As a last resort to get tenants out, pay them to leave. "I'll give you a month's rent in cash if you vacate in three days and leave the place clean." It takes that long or longer to get them out, and they could damage the place before they leave. Get them to sign a receipt, so you can write the payment off against your property income as a business expense.

46. Add this clause to your contract: "Buyer reserves the right to show property to prospective tenants before the closing." This lets you rent the house before closing and saves you making one or two months' house payments while you find a tenant.

47. Put both the legal description and the street address on your contract. If one is wrong, you can still have a valid contract. (Check with your attorney.)

48. If you wrote an offer saying "$80,000 purchase price, buyer to assume $60,000 mortgage," then the price is locked in stone. If you wrote, "Purchase price is $20,000 above the existing mortgage," and the closing took place several months later, any amount the mortgage was paid down (principal reduction) would go into your pocket.

49. You might include a "studder" clause in your mortgage the seller is carrying back. It might read, "Buyer may, at his or her option, skip one payment per year." (Check with your attorney.) You could justify it to the seller by explaining it will be used for unexpected vacancies.

50. If you are buying a property and the seller is carrying back a mortgage, include a first right of refusal in the event the mortgage is sold. You might want to buy it for the great yield (if the discount is high enough). You may decide to refinance the property, use the new lender's money to close out the old mortgage, and put the discount in your pocket. It gives you options.

51. It's a good idea to include in your offer, "Buyer to approve all new leases"; otherwise you might find some strange people in your property after the closing (like the seller's relatives).

52. If you made the closing date subject to getting a tenant, a motivated seller living in the house would show it for you and help you sell it to a tenant. Since the seller has an interest in the house (if carrying back a mortgage), he or she would help you find a good tenant.

53. Does your tenant have a waterbed? You can get insurance for waterbed damage liability from Maryland Casualty Company for about $25. Let the tenant pay for it, of course.

54. When you give a financial statement to a banker, your real estate can be at maximum value (lots of equity), but your cars should be at minimum value. (The banker can check those easily.) This will make your whole statement look conservative.

55. If you can, think of becoming a notary. When you print your business card that says, "I buy real estate," print on the back, "Good for one free notary service." Punch a hole in the corner so they can hang it on a small peg at home. It will make them keep the card. Think of anything in your business that could be a freebie. You might as well build your business at the same time you're buying real estate.

56. Anyone can now sell a loan to Fannie Mae. You may sell at full face value or, at worst, a small discount (depending on your interest rate). For information, write to: Fannie Mae, 3900 Wisconsin Avenue, Washington, D.C. 20016.

57. I heard of a man who makes a living writing who offers 75 percent of the asking price on all MLS listings over six months old. He gets turned down a lot, but he gets some great buys also.

58. When the seller gives you utility bills, count the meters on the property. The seller may give you the bills for two meters and actually be paying on three meters.

59. You can keep updated on home sales in your city by subscribing to "Existing Home Sales." It is published by the National Association of Realtors. It contains: housing affordability, condo and co-op sales, state-by-state resale volume, and prevailing sales prices in major metropolitan areas. It can alert you to a changing marketplace (sales volume going up or down dramatically). It sells for $48 to nonmembers and $32 to members. Write to:

> National Association of Realtors
> Economics and Research Division
> 777 14th Street, N.W.
> Washington, D.C. 20005

60. If you ever carry back a large mortgage on a property you're selling, say $100,000 or more, divide it into four $25,000 notes secured by one mortgage. If you ever need cash and have to sell it, you may only have to discount one-quarter of it instead of all. The smaller amount makes them easier to sell to private investors. You could offer them as down payments on four different properties. It gives you lots of options.

CHAPTER TWENTY-SEVEN

Questions I've Heard

After each of the hundreds of lectures I have given, the question-and-answer sessions usually last an hour or more. Some questions seem to be common in all areas of the country, and you hear them over and over again. In the interest of giving you a better understanding of where to direct your efforts, this chapter will share a few of them with you.

In this land of so much wealth and opportunity, why do most people fail financially?

Statistics bear this out. According to the Social Security Administration, about 98 percent of us will have little or nothing by the time we reach retirement years. Why does this happen? There are old sayings like, "People don't plan to fail, they just fail to plan." However, there is more to it. Have you noticed that the children of wealthy people don't seem to fail? Once created, wealth tends to be kept. This

215

wealth-building training is passed on from generation to generation.

Most people fail because they are trained to fail. From the time you are born, everyone you love and respect puts you on a financial train to nowhere. I'm talking about your parents, grandparents, teachers, friends, peers, everyone you look up to. What are you taught? Get a job, work all your life, and get the gold watch. Save your money for a good retirement. Pay your taxes, and if you want to invest, dabble in the stock market. That's the basic financial training in this country.

Does it work? There is a simple, foolproof test: Take a look at our senior citizens, because they've already lived it. For the most part, they're dead broke. They don't have two nickels to rub together. It's a national disgrace. If that's your battle plan, you are doomed financially.

What you must learn is that what you have been taught doesn't work. I was stopped by a young lady after giving a television interview, and she said, "I believe what you say; it just goes against everything my parents taught me." I asked, "How are your parents doing financially?" She said, "Terrible. They're barely making it." I said, "I know you love them, but consider the source of the financial advice."

To become financially successful, you must learn from people who are themselves financially successful. The first step to getting off a financial train to nowhere is to raise your level of awareness so that you see you are on the train. Otherwise, you'll never pull the emergency cord and get off.

To become successful, you must be different. A wise person once said, "Find out what everyone else is doing and don't do that."

You must learn to be out of step with the world. You buy when people are selling, and you sell when people are buying. It is your uniqueness that makes you wealthy, not your sameness.

Where should I invest?

Buy property in middle-class to upper-middle-class neighborhoods. Avoid the extremes. Don't buy in Beverly Hills neighborhoods, and don't buy in the ghetto. In Beverly Hills you can't get enough rent to make the house payment. In the ghetto you need a guard dog and a gorilla to collect the rent, and life's too short. Keep yourself in good, solid neighborhoods where you can attract good tenants who will like the area and stay with you for longer periods of time. These solid neighborhoods will tend to appreciate in value over the long term and give you large profits.

What kind of real estate should I buy?

You should buy residential income property right now because of the housing shortages in many areas of the country. Moving into the late 1980s and early 1990s this will get worse, not better. If you're buying homes in middle-class neighborhoods, buy the lower-priced homes. Not necessarily fixer-uppers, just lower-priced. If homes are $70,000 to $100,000, buy the $70s, not the $100s. The higher-priced homes tend to pull up the value of the lower-priced homes.

If you are buying apartments, you want to buy bread-and-butter rentals in the good neighborhoods. These are rents that the average working person living in that neighborhood would pay. Obviously, it varies from area to area in your city.

The number of units isn't critical; the rent structure of the units *is* critical. There is a lot of protection in buying the average. If times get very good, the people in the lower-rent apartments will want to increase their standard of living, and they will fill you up from that direction. If we hit a recession, the people in the higher-rent units will want to lower their costs, and they will drop down and fill you up from the other direction. It's a little like the tide going in and out. You pick up the surge in both directions. You will have different tenants depending on the economy, but the important thing is you will always have tenants.

Should I manage my properties?

I could write a three-word chapter on management: Don't do it. It's just not good use of your time. It's a mundane part of real estate investing, and it's very low paying. If you want to make $10 an hour, swing a paint brush and paint one of your units. If you want to make $500 per hour, write offers. Keep yourself buying real estate and not in management. If you're starting out part-time, like most people, you've only got eight or ten hours a week at the most (your job takes forty hours or more). If you buy three or four rental houses and try to manage, you'll be changing light bulbs, fixing things, answering complaints, and showing the houses to prospective renters. In fact, you'll be doing everything except building wealth.

Farm out management, and you'll build financial independence much faster. However, to be in compliance with the new tax law for allowable depreciation losses, you must maintain some involvement in management. Check with your CPA.

Should I live in my rental property?

On the surface, it seems like a good idea. The property would be easy to manage, and you could really look after it. Actually, it is a terrible idea. It is one of the worst mistakes the beginning investor makes.

The problem is that you're human. You can't live with people without becoming emotionally involved with them. Tenants become Jack and Joyce, not Mr. and Mrs. Jones. You can't raise Jack and Joyce's rent because they have a hundred reasons why they can't afford it, and besides you couldn't face them if you did it (you see them almost every day).

Show me a building where the owner has lived for five

years, and I'll show you a building that is at least two years behind the rent curve for the neighborhood. As an investor, you should look for owner-occupied buildings. They provide instant profits just by raising the rents up to market. Will the tenants move? Not likely. They would have to pay the same rent elsewhere.

How do you make money if there is no positive cash flow?

A lot of people think your profit (the money you make on your investment) is cash flow the building throws off. Actually, it's only a small part of it. Your rate of return is determined by five factors: appreciation, depreciation, equity buildup, cash flow, and cash invested. By buying an investment property with a conventional down payment, you can get a comfortable rate of return, even 60 percent per year, even though the cash flow is zero. With leverage, you can raise your rate of return to over 1,000 percent per year. This kind of return on capital can build wealth for you very rapidly. You can use the formula over and over again to calculate what you'll make on your future investments. Chapter 13 of my first book, *How To Make It When You're Cash Poor*, explains this in detail.

How do you invest if your credit is bad? Say you've had a recent bankruptcy.

You can start by understanding that conventional sources of borrowing are closed to you. Don't beat your head against a brick wall by going down to the bank or savings and loan association and trying over and over again to get them to finance your home purchase.

You also need to understand you can borrow a million dollars on real estate and have no one check your credit. Take FHA and VA loans. You have to qualify when you originate these loans; but since they are government-backed loans, you can assume by paying a fee of a few dollars and signing your name. The lender is not as concerned about how good a credit risk you are, because if you don't pay, the government will. Now, if the seller carries back the balance of the financing on the house and didn't check your credit (many of them don't), you could actually buy a house with an existing FHA or VA loan on it without having your credit checked.

The way credit works, when you have created hundreds of thousands of dollars in mortgages, people will want to lend you money. Banks love to lend money to people who don't need it. As you owe more and more, banks will start to call you to see if you would like to borrow some money. Basically, it's a game. Once you learn how to play it, you too can become financially independent.

How can a person begin building financial independence starting with absolutely nothing? Give me a specific example.

The first step is to buy a home. If you are renting an apartment, you can buy a home—it's as simple as that. You can have that home even though you have no down payment and you can't seem to save a dime. You can get a home even though your credit is bad. A simple solution is a lease with an option to buy. You lease a home for, say, two or three years, and a portion of your rent goes toward your down payment on the property. Look at your benefits. You have set up a savings account that is building up a down payment on the house with no extra money coming out of your pocket. (You were paying rent anyway, right?) The second thing is you get to move into the house you'll be buying. The kids aren't playing in the street anymore; you have a backyard. You get the physical benefits of home ownership right away.

Where can you find people willing to lease-option their houses?

You can find them almost every day in the Houses for Sale classified ads. However, I think a more fruitful place is the Houses for Rent column, for the simple reason that everybody there has a problem. They have a vacant house they're not living in that they have to make payments on. Would making two house payments for a few months put a strain on your budget? Give them a call. You have a win/win solution for them.

Is it true that the 1986 tax law wipes out the benefit of investing in real estate?

No. When they change the rules, you don't have to change games, just change the way you play the game. Quick profits through rent raises and resales (either through fixer-uppers or just raising below market rents) will be taxed at the new low rates. There will be low income taxes also on high returns on capital brought about by the purchase of discounted mortgages. Buying properties from distressed sellers and reselling them produces large profits. A little knowledge can make you a lot of money.

FOOD FOR THOUGHT

There is no good excuse for not investing in real estate and getting started building wealth. If you stand back and take a look at the problem objectively, the only person standing in your way is you. Why don't you get out of your own way?

CHAPTER TWENTY-EIGHT

Getting Started

Now that you have read concepts, ideas, and techniques that can make you a lot of money, the final hurdle is here—the physical process of getting started. You're excited after you've finished reading, and that won't be true weeks from now, even days from now. It's important that you turn your commitment into the day-by-day plan of getting the job done. It's an old cliché, but the journey of a thousand miles really does begin with a single step. This chapter lays out a battle plan.

SET YOUR GOALS

Go back into Chapter 2 and set finite, specific goals for yourself. Print them up and display them prominently in your home. Break down subgoals: how many phone calls you will make per week, how many offers you will write per month, how many properties you will buy per year.

Make it reasonable; you can always raise the figure later. Remember, it must be believable to you.

ELIMINATE DISTRACTIONS

Get rid of the things in your life that interfere with making money. Quietly drop out of the Saturday and Sunday football or baseball-watching sessions with your friends. Eliminate socializing with coworkers after work, especially during the precious summer months when you have several hours of daylight to work on properties. If you're a TV addict, you may simply have to make the dramatic gesture of pulling the plug from the wall and cutting it off with a pair of scissors. You can give it back to yourself after you own two or three properties. Remember, when you change your habits, you change your life.

TIME MANAGEMENT

Here is a time-management technique I was taught years ago that can virtually double your daily work output. Take 10 minutes at the end of each business day before you go home and make a list of the 10 most important items you have to work on tomorrow in order of their importance. (It doesn't have to be exactly 10.)

When you arrive at work the next day, sit down at your desk and start to work on item 1. If you have a cup of coffee when your first get in, take it to your desk and continue to work on the first item. If you hit a block (need some information or are waiting for a phone call), drop down to item 2 and start to work on it. If you're blocked on 2, drop to item 3. If 1 clears up, go back and work on it until you've finished.

Keep working on the most important thing you need to complete. You eliminate almost all the distractions in the workplace, and you'll find you are no longer shooting the breeze with your coworkers. Your efficiency level will shoot up, and—believe me—your boss will notice.

MONITOR YOURSELF

Go down to an office supply store and buy yourself the cheapest old ratty five-year diary you can find. Open the diary to the current date and log in the time you spent that day building financial independence (calling, driving neighborhoods, writing offers, etc.). Not work hours—that's earning a living. We're talking about wealth-building hours. Do that every day.

Every Sunday night add up the hours. This will give you a visual total of the time you have committed to changing your life. It should be eight or ten hours every week. If you keep it up, you're able to see results in a few short months. Remember, background and education are far less important than tenacity, the sheer determination to keep going. If you have that, you can make everything else work.

LAUNCH YOURSELF

Make a commitment, and make it a special occasion. Treat yourself to a nice dinner and perhaps a bottle of good wine. Toast your new venture. Go over the goals you have set during dinner. If you're married, you might decide who will work on what. You may have to experiment for a while, but you will soon find where the various strengths lie in the marriage. Adjust accordingly.

REWARD YOURSELF

The reward system is an important motivator. Take as your first reward something really juicy. Something you have always wanted. A trip, a cruise, perhaps that special fur. Set a goal and give yourself the reward.

For example, you could decide that when you have put together five transactions, you will get your reward. Then every transaction becomes one-fifth of something you have always wanted. When the reward gets close, instead of lagging, you will redouble your efforts to get there faster so you can enjoy it. How do you keep going afterward? Set a new goal and a new reward. It is much easier to get wealthy in stages.

Press on. I would wish you good luck, but somehow, I don't think you're going to need it. You'll be making your own luck from now on. When you're working smart, the harder you work, the luckier you get.

Index

227